Sales Management

Patrick Forsyth

MARKETING

04.10

- *The* fast track route to mastering all aspects of sales management

- Covers the key areas of sales management, from techniques for managing sales people at a distance to sales planning, and from assembling a top-flight team to staying market-focused

- Examples and lessons from benchmark companies in hotel management, financial services and pharmaceuticals

- Includes a glossary of key concepts and a comprehensive resources guide

>EXPRESS EXEC.COM<

essential management thinking at your fingertips

Copyright © Capstone Publishing 2002

The right of Patrick Forsyth to be identified as the author of this work has been asserted in accordance with the Copyright, Designs and Patents Act 1988

First published 2002 by
Capstone Publishing (A Wiley Company)
8 Newtec Place
Magdalen Road
Oxford OX4 1RE
United Kingdom
http://www.capstoneideas.com

CIP catalogue records for this book are available from the British Library and the US Library of Congress

ISBN 1-84112-193-2

Printed and bound in Great Britain

This book is printed on acid-free paper

Substantial discounts on bulk quantities of Capstone books are available to corporations, professional associations and other organizations. Please contact Capstone for more details on +44 (0)1865 798 623 or (fax) +44 (0)1865 240 941 or (e-mail) info@wiley-capstone.co.uk

Contents

Introduction to

ExpressExec

ExpressExec is 3 million words of the latest management thinking compiled into 10 modules. Each module contains 10 individual titles forming a comprehensive resource of current business practice written by leading practitioners in their field. From brand management to balanced scorecard, ExpressExec enables you to grasp the key concepts behind each subject and implement the theory immediately. Each of the 100 titles is available in print and electronic formats.

Through the ExpressExec.com Website you will discover that you can access the complete resource in a number of ways:

» printed books or e-books;
» e-content – PDF or XML (for licensed syndication) adding value to an intranet or Internet site;
» a corporate e-learning/knowledge management solution providing a cost-effective platform for developing skills and sharing knowledge within an organization;
» bespoke delivery – tailored solutions to solve your need.

Why not visit www.expressexec.com and register for free key management briefings, a monthly newsletter and interactive skills checklists. Share your ideas about ExpressExec and your thoughts about business today.

Please contact elound@wiley-capstone.co.uk for more information.

Introduction

Is sales management different from other kinds of management? Chapter 1 says that it is and identifies some of the ways in which it is special.

» A special form of management
» Key approaches to sales management

"In this business environment, satisfy the customer is a sacred cow. Even most car dealers are doing that. Sales managers and store managers everywhere are imploring their people to put the customer first. But they're only playing catch up. In the new world of commerce, satisfying is only the beginning ... So don't satisfy customers, everyone does that. Surprise them. Give them something they don't expect."

Robert Kreigel and David Brant

A SPECIAL FORM OF MANAGEMENT

Sales, and selling and the sales force, is inherently a part of the marketing mix. It must be deployed appropriately if it is to play its part and have a significant effect on the whole. That means that those people undertaking the sales task must be professional: able to communicate persuasively and create the necessary relationship with customers. It also means that the efforts of sales staff must be properly coordinated and therefore well managed: sales management is therefore important, and can directly influence results.

The management of any group of staff is important if they are to perform well. In sales there are a number of particular factors that make it especially so.

» *Isolation*: sales people must work predominantly on their own and there is a possibility that, without supervision, they become disassociated from the overall marketing effort and that their activity is therefore incomplete.
» *Geography*: sales people must work away from base, sometimes far away. Apart from the isolation referred to above, this means that applying management to them is inherently more difficult, and probably more time consuming than with staff in the office.
» *The nature of the task*: selling is a social skill, one that must be constantly fine-tuned if it is to do the desired job satisfactorily. Customer attrition can dilute such skills and management must act regularly to prompt sales people to maximize their approach in whatever way prevailing market conditions make necessary.

KEY APPROACHES TO SALES MANAGEMENT

Sales management is not simply a supervisory process, that is, in the sense of the "policing" role of management: checking and making sure things are done. It is, or should be, a creative role, one that enhances the ongoing sales activity and ensures it achieves everything possible. So too the relationship between sales people and sales manager should be a constructive one and viewed as such by both sides. Two other factors are of key importance.

» *Change and complexity*: the markets of the twenty-first century are nothing if not dynamic. For example: customers are increasingly demanding and fickle, distribution patterns are ever changing (e.g. with the increasing power of large customers and the e-sales routes now possible in many industries), buying processes and responsibilities change and pressure on time means buyers may want less personal relationships with suppliers.

» *Competition*: competition (including global competition) seems to increase all the time. There is a direct impact here on the sales job. Customers not only have considerable choice in almost any industry and product area one cares to mention, they have choices that are very close in performance, price, service and other factors. There has come to be a powerful commodity aspect to many markets. This means that sales people have a three-tier job to do. They must:

   » communicate (clearly and appropriately)
   » be persuasive
   » differentiate.

In other words it is not enough to be able to describe products and services effectively, nor even to do so persuasively – always there is the added dimension of ensuring something is described in a way that makes it more desirable than other similar products on the market.

Because of these factors the quality of selling itself can literally be a differentiating factor, giving any organization that maximizes its effectiveness an edge over competition. This is a vital factor in marketing success. The manager or managers who head up the sales function, and who work to make it effective, have a vital task. It is a complex job, and one that in future will tend to get more complex as the trends described here progress. For sales management, creatively making the sales activity work well is a challenge; for the organization an effective sales management function, now and in the future, is a must.

What is Sales Management?

Sales management is a part of strategic marketing. Chapter 2 looks at some of the ways, large and small, in which its role is significant.

» A management responsibility
» A fragile process
» Searching for an "edge"

"The joy of businessmen and women is to win – to create, lead, inspire and motivate teams of people who, by their creativity, speed of reaction, dedication and relevance to the needs of tomorrow, will ensure that their business gets in front and stays there."

John Harvey-Jones (All together now, Heinemann)

Despite the now long currency of the word marketing, there are still sometimes questions asked about the "difference between sales and marketing." Yet there should be no confusion. The days when marketing was regularly used as a euphemism for selling, or indeed advertising, are surely long gone. Selling, and the sales people who carry it out, are as inherently part of the individual techniques of marketing as is public relations, promotion or any other. And, to define sales management, it is the function – or person – responsible for creating and maintaining a suitable sales activity through management and supervision of the sales team (most usually the field sales team, rather than other categories of sales job), and hence achieving, through them, the required sales results.

In addressing sales management – what the sales manager must do and why – it is worth noting that in some organizations the sales function can be something of a neglected area, underrated and with other more glamorous techniques claiming more than their fair share of the limelight.

That is not to say that large numbers of organizations do not pay any regard to selling. Most do – to one extent or another. Certainly sales training is now much more likely to be used than was once the case, and there is a general acceptance of the need for excellence in selling as in so many other business and management techniques. Only through such an attitude can an organization look to thrive and prosper. Much of this concern is with the techniques of selling. These are, of course, important. Sales people must be able to deploy such techniques effectively and if they are up against a competitor that can do so better – more appropriately in whatever way – they may well lose out.

However, a broader view of selling must be taken if the overall effectiveness of the sales resource is to be maximized successfully. Specifically looking at the sales resource from a broader perspective means viewing it as essentially a marketing technique – one that needs to be regarded as a variable like any other. The sales resource must play an appropriate part in whatever overall marketing mix an organization decides to use (something that may well vary over time). And its doing so will not just happen. It needs planning. It needs organizing. Above all it needs regular fine-tuning if it is to act continuously to achieve planned results in the marketplace, and do so with some certainty.

A MANAGEMENT RESPONSIBILITY

It is an old saying that selling is too important to leave to the sales team. In many ways their likelihood of success is dependent on a wide range of things from quality of product or service, to company image, technical support and after sales service and customer care. Any success the team may achieve is certainly dependent on the way the organization – and thus whatever managers this necessitates (the sales manager, marketing manager, general manager in a smaller business or others) – views the sales resource. And on how they use it innovatively to create not just an efficient final link with the market but make sales an asset that can gain real competitive advantage in markets that are doubtless also targeted by competitors.

A FRAGILE PROCESS

Three other factors make this overall view of the sales resource vital.

Market change

In recent years markets have been nothing if not volatile. This has compounded increasing competitiveness, but such is an international fact of life. Everywhere all aspects of marketing are having to work harder if an organization is to hold on to, and develop, markets. It is said that sustainable competitive advantage comes only from innovation. We are in times when innovation is needed in many aspects of a company's operation: organization, product development – and that of sales is no exception.

Furthermore, one of the most pertinent changes of recent times has been with customers. They have had to react within their own organizations to protect and secure their future, and their attitudes to suppliers have changed markedly with any economic difficulty. The expectations of customers is now better defined than ever before: they know the service they want, the technical standards they want and they seek suppliers who can provide prompt and well matched answers to the problems of opportunities that initiate their purchase of anything – product or service. Not least, they want to deal with professional people representing a professional firm. And they want efficient support, response and communications throughout the relationship. Faced with any shortfall in their requirements they have absolutely no compunction about voting with their feet and going elsewhere.

In addition, buyer loyalty is less than in the past. Success on one occasion does not guarantee that people will buy again. Customers are demanding, fickle and need to be treated in just the right way. All this is not a momentary circumstance. Any lingering belief that "it will all be easier when things get back to normal" must be ruled out. Realistically circumstances are simply not likely to return to those of more straightforward or less competitive times. All organizations must all live with, and adapt to, changed circumstances.

The sales resource must be organized and must operate in a way that deals with the new realities. To do this requires more than "going through the motions," it means every detail of the process must be thought through and implemented in a way that creates the required edge.

Attention to detail

In terms of detail, prevailing standards often leave something to be desired. The best way to explain this is perhaps through an example, the personal experience of the author, that shows how such details can be missed or dealt with incompletely or ineffectively.

EXAMPLE

Some of my work is in the hotel industry. In one recent project, talking with a sales team about the sale of meeting and conference facilities (a major area of business for many properties) I touched on the use of photographs as a simple kind of sales aid. After all, if a prospective customer seeking a venue for a training course, a banquet or a wedding is shown into an empty room, as is often the way, then it is asking a good deal of them. They must imagine it laid out in just the way that will make their unique function a success. Realistically it is not a degree of imagination to be assumed.

All that was available was brochures produced a few years before, and just before the hotel first opened. These – presumably because the hotel was not yet operating at the time they were originated – showed only empty rooms; hardly a spur to the customers' imagination (and not so uncommon in the industry). Yet a suggestion that some money should be spent creating a small portfolio of new shots was rejected by the Sales Director with immediate concern for the budget.

So, it would have cost some money, though not too much. But the alternative was that many of their prospects, who are very likely to check out more than one venue, will find this particular aspect of the sale more impressive elsewhere. In a competitive business ignoring this kind of detail is simply to risk letting business go by default. This was in a five-star and well-known hotel.

The above example may seem to focus on an insignificant detail. Not so, it is precisely such things that can make the difference between getting agreement or not. Clearly if a number of such factors are similarly diluted in effectiveness, then a real disadvantage is created.

The reason for mentioning such an example as this is not to bemoan current standards in the hotel or any other industry; rather it is to show how such situations *create marketing opportunities*. Quite simply, those who get such details right, all of them, all the time, will do best.

Innovation

The example above focuses on an important detail, albeit one that is hardly novel in the industry mentioned. Beyond that kind of detail other more innovative factors may be added that also create an edge (even a strengthening is worthwhile) for those doing the selling. Such may either be an individual initiative, one that is the idea of an individual sales person, or something that is adopted by management for use throughout the team. One, of course, may lead to the other, though such initiatives must be appropriate to the individual customer and may not be suitable for use slavishly with every contact (a thought we return to later).

Again the example box below illustrates this further.

EXAMPLE

Here we look at a sales situation observed in a major international airline. A common problem in this industry is the need to brief and update travel agents. Not just the manager of such establishments – but all their staff who have customer contact and who might influence their customers' choice.

In this organization one particular salesman had evolved a well-proven approach to deal with this in major outlets in which the number of such people were greatest. He would arrive, by appointment, and with a tray of coffee and doughnuts bought at a nearby shop. He had persuaded his customer to allow him to convene an impromptu coffee break: a group of the staff gathered round and he had their undivided attention for 15–20 minutes. In a large outlet he would repeat this twice, or more, to accommodate all the staff yet prevent their service to customers from being decimated. It was a scheme that worked well for all concerned. It was also not easy to copy; possession is nine points of the law and he had set a precedent – you cannot have too many coffee breaks in the same morning and competitors found it difficult to deal with the situation in a way that was as productive for them.

This seems like precisely the sort of good thinking that should be endemic around a sales operation. It worked well because it took into account the needs of the customer and did not seek simply to get done what the sales side wanted. If such an idea suits even a small number of customers it is worthwhile (and other solutions must be sought with others).

This is certainly the sort of idea that can be developed by one person and then the experience can be circulated so that others in the organization can try it too.

SEARCHING FOR AN "EDGE"

Whatever aspect of the sales process one considers, it may potentially yield to an examination aimed at increasing the effectiveness of the process. If so the resultant success rate will be just a little better. The process is cumulative and, unless this is too strong a word, infinite. Certainly there are many opportunities to strengthen sales activity and ensure that the sales resource plays its full part as a major component of the marketing mix. In many commercial environments marketing can be seen as somehow "better" or more sophisticated than sales. Yet there is no reason for this; sales is a vital part of the marketing mix and one that is just as likely to provide opportunities to steal a march on competitors and impress prospects and customers alike as is attention to any other technique. As such it deserves the same degree of attention and creative thought lavished on other aspects of the marketing mix.

Against this background any organization must be clear what they want to achieve through sales, and similarly any sales manager must be clear what tasks they must focus on both tactically and strategically. The key sales management tasks are normally defined as:

» Planning
» Organizing
» Staffing
» Developing
» Motivating
» Controlling

The classic definition of management – getting things done *through* other people – underpins this and the objectives towards which this is applied are the achievement of specific, measurable largely economic factors: sales revenue and profit, and within that, detailed targets such as the product mix required and overall organizational measures such as return on sales and ultimately return on capital employed. Figure 2.1

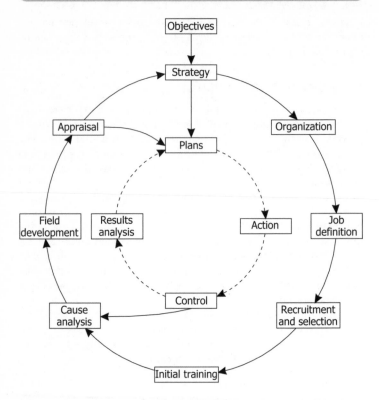

Fig. 2.1 Sales management long-/short-term tasks and responsibilities.

shows in graphic form the way sales management responsibilities must be exercised and the way different tasks relate (the detail of what must be done here is investigated in Chapter 6).

SUMMARY

The definition of sales management and the individual interpretation of what needs to be done are crucial to sales success. Successful sales management will:

» always rate sales as a key marketing variable;
» never underestimate the difference it can make to team performance;
» constantly keep abreast of market changes and customer expectations, matching operational practice to the real world accordingly;
» comprehensively define the sales job to be done, and work at ensuring that the detail that makes for sales excellence is addressed effectively and consistently; and
» always take a creative approach: recognizing that sales management is not there just to keep things operating efficiently, but to decide what constitutes efficient operation at any particular time. They know that change is the norm.

Evolution of Sales Management

Management is an ancient art. Chapter 3 comments and looks at the roots and development of modern sales management.

» Management in the round
» Sales management
» The last ten years

"There is no magic in management. I make sure people know what they are doing and then see that they do it."

Bob Scholey, Chairman of British Steel

Management as a generic activity has a long history. Modern remnants of projects such as the building of the pyramids provide ample evidence of management in action. It is not an unreasonable inference to suggest that many things before and since can be similarly regarded; without a degree of management cathedrals, canals and civilization itself would not exist.

MANAGEMENT IN THE ROUND

Yet, perhaps curiously, management, at least as a formal process worthy of study, is much more modern: it is a twentieth-century concern. And it is only late in the century that we find it becoming a matter of serious focus. Consider some dates.

1954

This year saw the publication of what many people would regard as the original "guru" guide to management: *The Practice of Management* by Peter Drucker (though there have been plenty more since).

1959

Though Harvard Business School in Cambridge Massachusetts had been in existence since early in the century, business schools only came to Europe in this year when INSEAD opened, and Britain lagged behind with both the London and Manchester Business Schools opening in 1965.

1965

From the sixties onwards management was increasingly a source of focus, indeed its study became both more formal, and increasingly also a matter of fad and fashion with a new "magic" technique seemingly arriving every week promising to be the ultimate panacea for success. Some – management by objectives (MBO) – effectively formalized common sense. Others – transactional analysis (TA) – utilized psychology in the cause of management. Some are long forgotten, though all perhaps helped focus peoples' minds and contributed to consideration of what did work best. The process continues. A few can, looking back, be viewed as milestones, for example the following.

1982

The book *In Search of Excellence* (Tom Peters and Robert Waterman) was not only a best seller and the purveyor of sound advice (and more acronyms, e.g. MBWA – management by walking about), but also a spur to the many more books, articles and a whole new consideration of the practical "best ways forward" that followed. By this time there was a general feeling that if not exactly a science, management was something that needed a considered approach and that a multitude of management techniques assisted its practice.

Certainly now as we head into the twenty-first century, things have quietened down in the sense that management is well accepted as necessary, as is the need to go about it in the right kind of way. Supposed "magic formulae" are treated with more skepticism, or viewed merely as useful – a way of prompting investigation and thought. The study of management-matters is, these days, predominantly practically based.

It should be accepted by all, however, that management does not, and never will, consist of a prescribed list of unfailingly "correct" methods and techniques. Rather it is time-dependent, that is it is something that changes over time with what is "right" being only a question of what works, today and in a particular context. And deciding what that is exactly needs care and judgment. Remember the view of H.L. Mencken who said "There is always a well-known solution to every human problem – neat, plausible – and wrong." This is certainly the case with a specialized form of management such as sales management.

SALES MANAGEMENT

The evolution of the sales management role is not complicated. Whenever there have been teams of sales people they have needed some form of direction. There are, however, circumstances and events that have influenced the way it is regarded and the way it operates. The prime reason for dwelling on this is that as times continue to be dynamic it is important for sales managers, and others concerned, to recognize changes that may have operational implications and to resolve to spot them early and act on them.

The chronology here is not of itself important (and is in some instances not intended to be precise); it does however put other comments in perspective.

Starting in the mid-twentieth century, we begin with the observation of major influences that operated over longer time periods.

1945

With the end of the Second World War, industry was left at a low ebb. The period thereafter was one of *recovery* in which a production orientation was pre-eminent. Making things was more important than selling them; if they could be made then, after the privations of the war, they could be easily sold.

1955–1965

Gradually production orientation gave way to one of marketing; it became important to ensure that what was being made would appeal to customers and that it could be sold. This was perhaps the *evangelical* period for marketing, a time when managers were recognizing and learning to take a market view.

1963

This year saw the publication of Vance Packard's seminal book *The Hidden Persuaders*, a message to consumers everywhere that they were being exploited, particularly that advertising influenced them in ways they did not realize (or at least that they should be aware of the "hard sell" directed at them from all parts of the marketing mix – including selling).

Also becoming active at this time was the American consumer champion Ralph Nader, whose initial efforts were directed at the motor car industry (and safety issues) but which spread to many other areas. These kinds of early influence have led to others and it is from all this that selling has had to deal with increasingly well-informed customers.

1965–1975

As competition intensified marketing moved into a *technique* period. During this period, management and marketing training expanded (aided in the United Kingdom by the way in which the *Industrial Training Act* of 1964 promoted training). Managers were under no illusions: they recognized that a professional approach was necessary to everything that would address competition, and produce an edge in the marketplace. Sales management was one of many marketing techniques that were viewed more and more professionally during these years as people strived to find what worked best. There was a parallel focus on the psychology of selling being developed at this time, with initiatives such as research done by David Mayer and Herbert Greenberg (e.g. What makes a good Salesman? *Harvard Business Review* July/August 1964) who brought the terms empathy and ego drive into considerations of selling.

Alongside the development of training, more and more began to be published about management, and in an increasingly accessible how-to style.

1970

During this year Mike Wilson's book *Managing a Sales Force* (Gower) was published. This was the most successful – and the best – of the new-style books about sales management. It had little in common with the dense textbook style of much previous management writing, or with the voluminous nature of the previous "bible" – US Dartnell Publishing's *Sales Managers' Handbook*. Its practical format was wholly accessible; packed with forms, charts and examples – it was seminal and provided a blueprint for successful operation (and also helped change the style of management books generally thereafter). From this time onwards sales management was recognized as a significant marketing component in its own right. The current edition of this book still provides a prime reference.

Mid 1970s

This was the starting point of SPIN. This is a trade marked term: Huthwaite International's research-based approach to sales training, which not only became a successful product (courses, packages and books are now available around the world), but was instrumental in getting selling taken much more seriously as an influential element in promoting marketing success, though much of the original premise here reflected what others already thought of as common-sense approaches. The spin (sic) this put on serious thinking about sales and sales management was important; selling – for long regarded as something "to do to people" – gradually began to be practiced in a way that more closely reflected customer needs.

Mid/late 1970s and beyond

A market trend began around this time that was to change sales management for evermore. Customers no longer formed one group – larger and smaller customers began to be regarded as being different in *nature* as well as size. The world of selling was suddenly full of people with titles such as Major Account Manager and Key Account Executive and sales management had to organize more diverse sales teams in the recognition that different customers needed differing sales approaches. Indeed customers took action to put power into their buying – for example forming the buying groups that are now common in many industries.

Similarly inflationary pressures in many markets also began to exert a pressure for change that reduced or controlled costs involved in sales forces and the way they were organized and managed. For example, the increased cost of keeping field sales people on the road led directly to experiments that resulted in the successful development of telephone selling – a development that, in turn, led directly on to the call centers of today. (These are now ubiquitous in many industries and were pioneered in some such as banking.)

THE LAST TEN YEARS

Like so much else in business and management the IT (information technology) revolution has had a considerable effect on selling and sales management (see Chapter 4, The e-dimension). Here we limit examples to two main areas.

» The electronic revolution has changed a great deal about the way people do business. Sales people have to deal with organizations in which the computerized stock control system has replaced "the buyer" to some degree and meetings are harder to get. The speed of transactions has increased dramatically – sales people can check details for a buyer from a mobile computer as their discussions proceed. Speed, precision and detail are the order of the day and saying: *"I'll check with the office and get back to you"* may be regarded as prohibitively old-fashioned and slow.

» Information has changed radically also. Sales people must file much data: sales, travels, customer details, competitive intelligence and more. For the most part this is no longer filled in on forms and posted to the office; it is entered into some sort of electronic data collection system and is available instantly to sales management making decisions. Tactical changes should be easier.

» Buyers are increasingly professional. This means they are better, and more specifically trained, better informed (and this is increasing as buyers make use of the Internet and other developments to help with pre-purchase research). Underestimating the knowledge or ability of buyers is now not just unwise, it can be fatal.

Some developments linked more than one of these factors. The concept of Major Customers and the availability of electronic systems have given rise to new techniques of CRM – Customer Relationship Management. This is, in some respect, no more than the process good sales people used years ago – but it is formalized, systematic and comprehensive. And, in electronic form, it is fast, precise and instantly transferable. It handles the basics: reminding a sales person to renew a contact, for instance. And it does things previously impossible.

If a customer in London refers a sales person to their opposite number in Singapore, then the right person in the Singapore office can be on the telephone to them without delay – and with all the facts and figures they would expect at their fingertips. Systems are worth checking out. Their data collection role is important, and mean that sales people can operate from a base of much more precise, up to date and comprehensive information than was the case in the past. They can be customized (indeed you should never even contemplate using something that does not match your customer situation).

Essentially the changes here relate as much to selling as to sales management. Sales management is, as you would expect, influenced by the people they manage, their role, the circumstances prevailing within the organization and outside it in the market. And, if you want to nail it to one thing, then that is the fact that sales management, like selling, must be customer focused to be successful.

Postscript

Two other changes are worth noting. Both are difficult to date as they have crept up on us. One is certainly significant: staff expectations of management have changed. It must be much more consultative than was the case years ago, managers must find a way of dealing with people that is both acceptable and effective. It may also be wise to keep a wary eye on such factors as employment legislation. Many would say that managing people has become more time consuming. Perhaps. If so, then the response is surely to intensify the focus on key issues and ensure that new tasks are given priority.

The second change is perhaps more frivolous. In this politically correct world, the word salesman (which used to define field sales personnel as opposed to those in other sorts of sales position) has become unacceptable. Salesperson is the order of the day – even if it seems to encompass people as diverse as the shop assistant and the major account manager – thus bringing field sales person into the vocabulary. It does illustrate in yet another way the need for everyone to keep up with changes of all sorts!

SUMMARY

The moral for today's sales managers is clear.

» Focus on three levels: your job, the sales team's job and the customers' expectations.
» Watch for change: there is no one right way of managing in this area, much less one that will be correct, as is, for ever.

» Link what is operationally possible and necessary to the organization's objectives and goals: the activity of the sales team is a means to an end – how it must be prompted to go about its job depends on the objectives and the market. So sales management solutions must be practical for the team and the organization and yet always create acceptance and satisfaction with customers, on whom all marketing success ultimately depends.

The E-Dimension

IT affects every nook and cranny of business. Chapter 4 shows that sales management is no exception.

» Some dangers
» Opportunities
» Best practice

"If your system works well, it's obsolete."

Anon.

Information technology in all its forms is changing the face of business. Marketing ranks high amongst those areas affected – or taking advantage of this. Some benefits come from very sophisticated systems. An example given in the book *Wired Life* (Charles Jonscher, Bantam Press) makes a point. A typical major airline may have ten different fares for people flying on the same flight (one of thousands of flights made each day). United Airlines have pioneered the use of computers, using probability analysis, applied statistics and econometrics, to analyze past records of bookings, cancellations and fares to formulate policy for fare setting and discounting in a way that maximizes the number of fare paying passengers and the returns made.

However, sales management and sales consist primarily of personal interactions. But it would be a mistake to believe that this leaves them untouched by the information technology and e-commerce revolution. There are already many implications and doubtless more to come; this is an area of fast change. Here we touch on key factors and some of the ways in which these affect the job of keeping a field sales team functioning effectively.

SOME DANGERS

Taking certain negative factors first, consider the customer. They are as affected by the march of technology as you are, and what technology does for them may actively make life more difficult for you. Two examples illustrate.

» *Customer ordering systems* are now often automated. At a supermarket checkout the till rings up the money for the customer but it also records the resulting stock level. At a particular point the computer initiates a new order to the supplier and further supplies are delivered. Much of the process in between may be automatic. Then, later, a sales person is on the supermarket's doorstep asking to see the buyer. What's the reaction? Someone might say *"our computer buys your product"* and a meeting is declined. The sales person has a list of things they want to discuss: product positioning, new promotion, display and merchandising opportunities – all these could be delayed or go by the board. It makes the job of selling that much more difficult and specific steps have to be taken to make the wanted meeting seem attractive – unmissable – to the buyer.

» *Products* are getting more and more *sophisticated*. Sounds good, but this probably actually means more complex. This in turn means more product information for sales people to take on board and then put over to customers, clearly and quickly (customers will not make more time for your people because they are slow, or circuitous, in explanation). This has clear implications for briefing and training – more information, more regular changes and updates. But it is an opportunity nevertheless: if sales people take all this in their stride the impression they make on people is enhanced. It is doubly useful to make sure they excel at anything competitors find difficult.

Overall, in some industries e-commerce is taking over from, or being added to, other forms of distribution. So far the things sold most successfully over the internet are limited and fall into comparatively few categories. These include:

» price driven purchases (often where the product is checked out elsewhere and only bought over the Internet);
» enthusiast products (e.g. computer games);
» convenience (e.g. buying a book that then lands on the doorstep); and
» niche products of various kinds.

The range may well widen. Meantime management must ensure that where personal selling remains possible, acceptable – even wanted – it is well deployed. It is perfectly possible to persuade some customers that it is better (for them) to buy following personal, individual advice than just by scanning a computer screen. Sales people need to be aware of the environment in which they operate, and the fact that the "buying experience" that people participate in now includes a greater variety of processes than ever before.

Although there are dangers in many of the other factors now mentioned, the primary impact is positive and the moral is the same in all cases – get these things right and you add to any edge between your organization and team and their competitors.

OPPORTUNITIES

There are many ways in which technology interacts with sales. For the manager the job is to see the possibilities, and to take a broad view of them. Some of the questions that must be asked of a possible new initiative are as follows.

» What will it cost?
» What effect will it have on productivity?
» How will it affect peoples' sales power?
» Will it have a positive or negative effect on customer service and perceptions?
» Will it assist in building relationships and business?

These different factors need balancing carefully. Something may seem to cost too much, but there may be dangers in ruling it out and missing significant benefits. Two improvement areas must be assessed: productivity and sales effectiveness. About the first Stanley Roach, Chief Economist of Morgan Stanley, said *"The productivity gains of the information age are just a myth. There is not a shred of evidence to show that people are putting out more because of investments in technology."* Harsh words, and in the sales area not borne out – but careful checks are needed to make sure that a positive effect will accrue from any technological changes contemplated. Assisting productivity may make something immediately desirable, but how will customers see it and what will it do to their perception of your customer service? It is this aspect that influences sales effectiveness most.

The following examples, in no particular order of importance, illustrate the range of areas to consider here and hint at further changes to come.

» *Mobile telephones*: a simple one first. These are already ubiquitous and their use can certainly boost customer service and speed things up; but they should *never* ring and interrupt a customer meeting. They seem headed to duplicate some of what computers do, though how well they will do so remains to be seen.

» *Mobile computers*: these, in the form of everything from high capacity laptops to simpler handheld devices (e.g. Palm or Psion machines), can go into the customer meeting with the sales person. They allow a variety of things to be done quickly and easily:
  » checking stock and placing an order for a customer from their own office during the visit;
  » updating records or issuing instructions to the sales office (perhaps from the car after a meeting); and
  » forming part of a presentation to a customer (using PowerPoint charts to explain complex figures perhaps).

  The net impact here should be good: saving time, adding immediacy and allowing informed decisions to be made on the spot.

» *Assisted learning*: a variety of skills can be put over by learning packages (e.g. programmed learning devices on CD-ROM). This may be useful for product knowledge or sales skills, though remember that teaching the interactive skills deployed during sales meetings may need other inputs too.

» *Communications*: methods have changed (when did you last get a telex or even a fax?) and e-mail has replaced many more complex messages. It takes time to get something written, printed out and posted, so the convenience is obvious. But it is not right for everything. An e-mail may fail to impress a customer because it is so informal, or so brief it fails to be clear. And it can be wiped out at the touch of a button (so may not produce any potentially lasting memory jogger with a customer), and it does not impress graphically in the way a company letterhead should. Horses for courses – a variety of methods must still be used, and sales people always going for the easy option may dilute the overall and cumulative impression they should be helping to build.

» *Research and information*: information is power it is said. Going to a meeting under-informed and showing that no trouble has been taken to find out about a new potential customer can quickly do damage. A while ago a few minutes on the telephone, with reference books or spent getting hold of a company's annual report was worthwhile. Now the ability to access the Website of so many organizations speeds and simplifies the whole process – though more than just this may be necessary, and sales people do have to actually *note* information obtained and think about how it can help them sell. Some rules and guidance from management here may be valuable. Websites are similarly a good way to gather competitive intelligence.

» *CRM (Customer Relationship Management) Systems*: here there is considerable sophistication with many different software systems available to record, monitor and prompt action with major customers. The data available here is invaluable, but the mistake should not be made of thinking that the system will do it all. Contact is personal and whatever prompt is given to the individual sales person they must interpret it sensibly and take appropriate action. Like many areas of systems a specific element of danger here is a lack of flexibility, with the system being followed slavishly and action directed at individual customers not being sufficiently well tailored.

» *Presentations*: in some industries the sales process involves the regular use of formal presentations (another important personal skill), and in these and in many meetings visual aids are often very professional looking; anything *ad hoc* can look slapdash. Such aids are important in assisting and augmenting customers' imagination; they must *support* what is said, however, and not take over the process. If well used they add an important additional dimension to the sales process; if not they can lull the sales person into ceasing to think sufficiently clearly; they go through the presentation on automatic pilot led by the charts or whatever they are using.

» *Your Website*: sales people have always had to link precisely with other media, they must build on the image of the organization and take the customer further in terms of both information and image. The many organizations that have Websites now have an additional element to assist in informing customers, and this may mean that by the time they talk to a sales person they are better informed than in the past (and this includes the information they have about competition, competitive prices etc.). A good Website can thus make the job easier for sales people, but even small deficiencies can cause problems (e.g. if it is difficult to navigate or manifestly not kept up to date). There are specific ways also that customer visits to Websites can be used to enhance the sales process.

  » *Research*: information can be gathered by prompting customers or enquirers to complete information (without making it mandatory or too onerous to do). A well-designed Website can thus provide ongoing, up-to-date information about customers – their feelings, requirements and more.

» *Telephone link*: software (or support) is available now to link customer visits to direct contact. A customer visiting a Website and wanting to take things further can click on a box and prompt telephone contact. Systems can ensure this happens promptly – or even guarantee that it happens so quickly that a call is received while the customer is on-line: they can look at information on screen while talking to a sales person.

The possibilities here are broad and varied. Any technology used alongside sales contact must be well thought out. It must be customer oriented and enhance customer service and satisfaction rather than just improving the basis for selling and the likelihood of success (though it should do this too!).

There are other implications here also. These include: selling overseas (where immediacy and quality of contact can be improved), and demonstration of commitment (a customer may be impressed by the contact provided by a Website in the same way as they may see advertising support making their job of selling on a product easier). Further technological developments will extend such possibilities. Already smart cards are allowing information to be collected about customers and linked to future contact and promotion and sales. For example, a customer's purchase of a particular product (paid for on a card) can be followed by sending them linked promotional material – a sales pitch to the shop where this happens may include reference to this kind of process.

BEST PRACTICE

Finally, let us consider examples of the cross over between personal and technological selling, first two simple ones – good and bad – from my own observation.

» *Good*: Recently I contacted Oberoi Hotels in India. It was easy to search for their Website and easy too to put a question to them through it. An hour later I had a call from their representative in

London. They had a fresh, warm lead to follow up, but from my perspective as a customer they already knew something about me and tailored their approach well to the circumstances, making it seem like excellent service. This kind of thing now represents the simplest kind of technological enhancement; yet the effect on the customer is good, the chances of prompting business enhanced. In such circumstances if the next stage for the supplier is going to visit someone, then that meeting should be just a little easier to handle and make persuasive.

» *Bad*: Recently I was visited by a financial services salesman (whose organization had better remain nameless). He arrived on time and seemed very professional, yet proved so highly dependent on technology that I rather lost patience with him. He disrupted my desk with his equipment – a laptop – and took me through a seemingly endless PowerPoint presentation the bulk of which was clearly standard, when the whole purpose of the meeting was to link individually to my circumstances. The effect was the reverse of what was intended. While the charts shown looked good, their message was distanced from the customer, and the proportion of the total message that came straight off screen diluted the impression that the salesman made in a business where personalities and their expertise are crucial. Moral: in selling, technology must always *support* the personal presence.

In both these cases the implications for sales management are clear. In the first, things seem to have been well organized with the customer in mind. The system worked and the individual sales person encountered had clearly been briefed as to how to work so that the separate effects on customers of what they did, and what the system did, enhanced one another.

In the second, technology seemed to have taken over, the salesman proceeded on automatic pilot, as it were, and the net effect made a sale less likely than it might have been. This was not because the technology could not have been organized to enhance matters, it could. Rather that insufficient thought had gone into deciding how the integration would be made; surely a sales management responsibility.

The modern sales manager now has the bigger job of organizing not just people, what they do and how they do it, but also the considerable technology used in whatever way to back them up. The whole needs to work well together, and no element of it can be left "just to happen," or the customer ends up with an experience that works less well for them.

SUMMARY

These trends are set on a course. The full implications are, perhaps by definition, unclear. Writing in *The Information Age* Manuel Castells stated:

> "The twenty-first century will not be a dark age. Neither will it deliver to most people the bounties promised by the most extraordinary technological revolution in history. Rather, it may well be characterized by informed bewilderment."

Fair comment. Technology may still perhaps be in its infancy. But already managers must be careful to take the right view of it – and to take the right action about matters it affects. The three key rules should be to:

» *take the broad view*: information technology does not effect just one, easily defined and self-contained area, it potentially affects *everything*;
» *seek opportunities*: but remember, changing technology does not automatically mean "new = good," changes may present difficulties too and it is as well be on your guard for them; and
» *give priority to customer focus*: just because something is technically possible does not mean it will create positive advantage; ultimately it is the effect on customers and on customer service that matter most. Checking things out is as important as moving ahead fast.

The Global Dimension

The world may be shrinking in some senses, but great distances are involved. Chapter 5 looks at the ''on the ground'' implications for sales management of global marketing.

» International options
» A little local difficulty
» Best practice

"The biggest wasters of their own resources are the people who don't know who they want to be or where they want to go."
Tom Hopkins, Sales trainer and author of "How to Master the Art of Selling"

For many years a slogan used by the UK Chartered Institute of Marketing (which interestingly grew from the Sales Managers Association) was – *The World is our Market*. Certainly an organization's sales activity is necessarily going to be different if it is being directed at customers on the other side of the world; sales management reflects these differences. A business may be successful on a limited geographical scale, for instance operating only in one major city. At the other end of the scale there are multinational businesses that span the globe; witness the posters you see having landed at almost any airport in the world, names such as Coca Cola, McDonalds, Ford, Hewlett Packard, Compaq and many more appear everywhere.

The task of sales management in the context of international business is to try to get as close as possible to the operational situation in the home market, i.e. to maximize the effectiveness of the sales role despite the geographical differences and distance involved.

INTERNATIONAL OPTIONS

To review this we need to consider the various ways in which international business can be organized.

Export marketing

This is selling goods to overseas customers but doing so from a base in your home market. Essentially this implies physically shipping goods across the world. This may be done by the organization themselves: for example using their own fleet of trucks to ship goods to Europe or beyond. It may be dependent on the use of shippers, whether goods are to travel by road, rail, air or sea. It can be done with no support or presence in the final market; but is an area that demands specialist knowledge of such things as export documentation, shipping, insurance, credit control etc. as well as marketing.

Sales management implications: with no people on territory, sales people must communicate with customers in a variety of ways. Continuity is important and with modern communications it should be easy to keep in touch. Almost always however, the basis of the customer relationship will be stronger if they are seen personally – visiting the territory – as well. Costs may prevent this being a frequent occurrence, but – despite the need to keep potentially high costs within bounds – visits must be organized that meet customer needs and sales staff need to be selected for this and briefed accordingly.

Export with a local presence

The form that a local presence takes clearly affects the way a company operates and thus the nature of the operation involved. Maybe the company will have:

» *their own local office*. This will link with the headquarters and may handle independently a range of things that have to be done locally (and maybe done differently from the way they are executed at home); local advertising or service arrangements, for instance.
» *An agent or distributor*, in other words a local company that undertakes the local work, and marketing, on behalf of the principal. Such a company may specialize, only selling, say, construction machinery. Or they may sell a wide range of products, sometimes across the whole range of industrial and consumer products in the way large distributors – often called trading houses in some parts of the world – do. Sometimes such arrangements are exclusive, meaning they will not sell products for competing manufacturers; sometimes not. Payment of such entities is often on a basis of results, but they cannot simply be set up and left to get on with it. Success is usually in direct proportion to the amount of liaison, support and communications that is instigated between the two parties by the principal.

Sales management implications: an active approach is necessary. For example, the distributor's sales staff must understand the product and know how to sell it. A company may well see this as an area for support: for example, they might provide training, flying trainers out onto territory and taking any other action necessary to make it work (translation of materials, perhaps). A distributor's sales staff must be influenced almost as much as a company's own sales team (though their people are not employees of the principal). Again ongoing communication needs organizing, as do regular visits.

International marketing

This implies a greater involvement in the overseas territories, everything from setting up subsidiaries, to joint ventures and, in some businesses, local manufacture. The complexities here can become considerable, with components, for example, being sourced from several different locations around the world, assembled in one or more main centers and then distributed to and sold in many markets. Such is common, for instance, in the motor market.

Sales management implications: whatever the nature of the local set up – its ability to field an effective sales activity is paramount. On a large scale a local sales force and all that goes with it is simply duplicated, i.e. a local force in a number of markets, and all need to be operated and therefore managed effectively. The overall marketing strategy must be reflected by sales force operations territory by territory.

Licensing

This is an example of one of the other approaches possible. Here nothing is done on an ongoing basis by the principal. They sell the right – the license – to produce the product to someone else. The deal may include help with a variety of set up processes (from the provision of drawings to machinery), but thereafter the local company runs their own show, and marketing, and payment is on some sort of "per product produced" basis.

Sales management implications: despite the distancing involved here revenue success will still depend on the quality of sales involved. So the "parent" company may want to secure and agree an involvement, even if it is no more than positioning the sales manager as a technical advisor. This is especially so when the returns to the principal are calculated, even in part, on sales results.

There are other methods also: for instance *franchising*, well known from the likes of McDonalds and Holiday Inn, but used with a wide range of products and services. Marketing's job is to select and use methods appropriately; and maybe to originate new ones. All such may need or allow the opportunity to influence the sales activity "on the ground."

A LITTLE LOCAL DIFFICULTY

Throughout industry, some companies sell what they produce in similar form world-wide. Others tailor the product to individual markets – even something as simple as a chocolate bar may have many different recipes and flavors for each of many different markets. This applies to many aspects of a product: cars may need change to meet local safety standards, books need translating, electrical products may have to work with different voltages etc. Check major brands, *Fanta* will be a different color of orange and a different taste depending on where you drink it. It can simply be arrogant to assume no change is needed, so marketing logically demands consideration of such options and that adaptations are made as necessary.

Similarly in sales, the marketing principle of "knowing your customer" is clearly paramount in overseas markets where people, culture, customs and more may be very different. Such differences will not only potentially affect details relating to the product, for example a number may be popular in one country and regarded as unlucky in another (as eight is regarded as auspicious by the Chinese), but also the manner of doing business. Here such things as the prevailing practice regarding negotiation, business ethics or time scale may all be different. Even a name – of a company or product – may need careful checking; what sounds catchy in English may be lewd in German or hilarious in Urdu.

There is thus a prime requirement for all sales staff, and their managers, that is that they strive to understand and adapt and accommodate when dealing with overseas markets.

For example things will not be the same at home and overseas. At home base a manager may inhabit a large office, surrounded by staff and support services. Someone operating in or visiting a different country may be one of a handful of people there. Posting a letter may mean going to the mailbox personally. Briefing a major customer may mean a visit "up country" in a four-wheel drive vehicle on roads made treacherous by the rainy season.

There are differences that will affect people very personally. Extremes may involve sales people politely eating sheep's eyes in the Middle East or trying to remember the etiquette involved in a meeting to negotiate terms, taking place in Japan. Beyond difference, you might also like to consider discomfort or even hostility. Some countries are not an automatic choice for comfort – a range of things: climate, politics, law and order – or lack of it – or simply inaccessibility may make them unattractive either as places to visit or to live. But if such are part of your market then you must staff them with people who can cope. Management must find people right for these tasks, and manage them too, bearing in mind that they must be highly self-sufficient.

BEST PRACTICE

The example commented on below links the global nature of business and of customers with new technology. It focuses not on one company, but on a particular industry, that of publishing.

Assuming you have this text in book form – where did you buy your copy? Maybe in a traditional book shop. Maybe in a specialist outlet, perhaps from a professional management institute or the direct ordering service of a newspaper or magazine. Or perhaps on line – operations such as Amazon (supposedly the best known e-business world wide) now take a significant proportion of total book sales.

Traditionally publishers' sales teams have been geographically organized. A bookshop, or wholesaler (supplier to smaller retail outlets), is visited by the sales person covering the area in which it is situated. In the home market this might be one of a team of directly employed people, overseas a sales person employed by a distributor. The only variance of this has related to size, with a major chain of shops buying centrally being dealt with by a senior person (the industry's equivalent of the Major Accounts Manager).

Now there is a new breed of customer to deal with. Amazon are not alone, but one of many such e-tailers selling books alongside a variety of other goods (as an example, UK operators – though their customers may be located elsewhere – include BOL and The Good Book Guide). Their business is worth a good deal to many publishers.

Research, carried out for the Singapore Publishers Association, shows that these kinds of organization:

» will not see everyone and who they do see is determined by their overall image of a publisher, which is influenced in turn partly by their ongoing communications (everything from catalogues to telephone calls);

» want advance information – and are concerned only with *their own* time scale;

» depend a great deal on *which individual* they see from a supplier; if they rate someone as unprofessional, uncaring or simply not sufficiently efficient then they will do less business (or see someone else); knowledge and operating approach and style is important;

» may demand that one publisher liaises with a number of people their end if a range of books and topics spans their organization (e.g. different buyers for general fiction and science fiction);

» expect accurate information and resist hype (if something is oversold, next time a different line will be taken); and

» have mandatory criteria that form part of their negotiation (e.g. they will not buy a new book without seeing the jacket).

It is the sales manager's job to check out the specifics of such a situation and organize and then maintain the contact that these new style customers want and like. Better still to do so in a way that satisfies them more than competition. If it needs some non-traditional approaches so be it. If it needs changes to procedures (e.g. book covers available further ahead of publication than usual) again so be it. Any organization that fails to discover and respond to this sort of market change is in trouble.

Those that do may be quoted as examples of best practice today. Tomorrow? That is another matter. Anything to do with selling and customer relationships is inherently fragile. It demands flexibility and that an eye is constantly kept on the ball.

SUMMARY

The key things here are to:

» *seek opportunities widely*: then organize to exploit them carefully and recognize that you must pace such development; things usually take longer when distances are involved;

» *identify and respect cultural differences*: and ensure that operations are organized to cope with them; and
» *regard communications as key*: overseas markets and the customers in them can easily be left feeling isolated, neglected or ignored; regular constructive contact is essential and some of it must be face to face.

The State of the Art

Sales management is a big job demanding a balanced approach and attention to detail. Chapter 6 reviews the key tasks.

» Planning
» Organizing
» Staffing
» Developing
» Motivating
» Control
» Looking ahead

"The underlying principle of all development, is practice."
James Allen, author of The Mastery of Destiny

Sales management is a generic skill. Its nature, importance and relationship with other activities are reviewed elsewhere in this work. Here the focus is on the day-to-day sales management process, and this in turn relates to the nature of the sales activity in a particular organization. In *Sales Force Management* (6th edition, McGraw-Hill; Churchill, Ford, Walker, Johnston and Tanner) it is said:

> "Selling is important, not only because of the company's immediate need to generate revenue through the sale of products and services, nor only because sales is the largest marketing expense, but also because the future of the company depends on sales people who can ... find more, win more, and keep more through carrying the voice of the customer throughout the firm."

It goes on:

> "Managing the selling function is one of the most important management functions in any firm, not just because selling is so important, but also because managing selling is unique."

Overlong sentences apart, this is fair comment. Sales management is important, and it is unique amongst management tasks.

While it is a process that must be applied differently in different organizations, industries and circumstances the key tasks are the same for all. These are:

» planning
» organizing
» staffing
» developing
» motivating
» control.

Each of these is reviewed in turn, with examples illustrating certain aspects of them and a link to current problems, issues or opportunities.

PLANNING

Planning is no academic nicety. Plans should drive the business, and the thinking that goes into planning is key to analysis and making sure that the activity reflects the real world. Essentially planning comes down to four key questions:

» where are we now? (analysing the current situation);
» where are we going? (demanding the setting of clear objectives);
» how will we get there? (this produces an action plan, setting out who will do what and when); and
» how will we know when we have got there? (the process of measurement and control).

These are no more than common sense, but they should prompt specific action by the manager in charge of the sales team.

Setting sales objectives

This process demands looking back and then forward. It is important that detailed and current information forms the basis of any extrapolation. Sales revenue will no doubt be clear, but detailed statements are needed in terms of areas like:

» sales by product
» sales by customer category
» sales in different areas; and
» sales linked to price (at different discounts and levels of profitability, for example); and more.

With this in mind, sales can be forecast, and this should be done in a way that recognizes and anticipates any changes that the forthcoming period will bring (it is not just a case of adding an attractive percentage increase). The next stage is to see *how* such a target can be met – this leads to the sales plan.

The sales plan

The key questions here are as follows.

» *What is to be sold*? (the detail, product by product as necessary): product mix is the key variable here. Depending on the product or service range, its positioning and design, direction may well be necessary for the sales force – it may be that the items to which they give priority, perhaps because they are easiest to sell, are not the company's priority – with other lines having higher profitability. Clarity is needed here, and leaving the mix sold just to "happen" should not be one of the options.

» *To whom?* (a statement that should reflect all categories of customer): here there may need to be plans for customers by category, or even by individual customer. Large customers may need to have strategies developed for them, especially where they have several different buying points (e.g. people, functions, geographic locations); this may be best thought of on a matrix basis.

» *At what price?* (recognizing the complexities of pricing policy): a logical pricing policy is necessary here, together with any discount structures that are necessary. Price is a marketing variable, but one of the places pricing policy must be implemented and work well is at the sales interface with the customer. The sales manager should be involved with decisions about pricing policy and must put the sales people in a position to work with the details effectively. Factors such as what independent authority sales people have to negotiate price and terms should be clearly understood by all.

» *By what methods?* (detailing how sales will be organized): the plan must specify sales actions very clearly. The mix of customers and the different levels and style of service they may want must be matched with the organization's intention to push for sales. The system must categorize customers, assign call frequencies, allow time for any necessary activity such as prospecting or telephone contact (and administration) and prompt a practical array of activity. It is little good aiming for sales results with no clear idea how they will be obtained or the scale of the effort required.

» *At what cost?* (and also with what cost-effectiveness): the sales plan has a cost, so budgeting is one aspect here. Sales productivity is the other concept that needs addressing here. Analysis of the ratio of sales to sales cost is just the starting point. Other measures may include: sales per territory, number of customers managed by a sales person, number of calls made per person (and on average per day), time spent face to face, average order value, strike rate – orders to call ratio, most successful sales person compared with the average (there can be a very significant gap here). There are details here worth constant vigilance and fine-tuning.

A significant part of many organizations' sales plans is the development of individual *customer strategies*. These sub plans can include profitability analysis, and set out details of action over a period across a complex organization with multiple buying points, matching this to internal considerations including product mix. This then becomes the basis for prompting and checking action. An example relating to this appears in the In practice section).

With the foregoing methodology in mind certain key practical points are worth emphasizing:

Key issues

» *Comprehensive sales plans*: plans must be activity as well as results based, and targets must link to both. Thus targets must be set not just for sales figures but for the activities that potentially produce them, e.g. prospecting, calls, meetings, proposals etc. As business approaches change new activities may become important and need adding in to the planning process.

» *Realistic targets*: the link between forecasting and planning must be sound. Whatever objectives the organization sets, at the level of individual sales person, targets must be achievable – they can, and perhaps should be challenging – but they should be achievable. Sales managers must increasingly be involved at senior levels of marketing planning to get this right.

» *Making the plan match real life*: in years past sales people had a territory, period. Now plans need to reflect a number of issues beyond geography, such include: product range, markets and different kinds of customer and buyer. A matrix approach is often the answer.

ORGANIZING

Organization addresses the basic design of the sale resource. First, it must be decided how many sales staff are needed. This is best done on a workload analysis basis, looking at the level of customer service required, the number of calls that will need to be made and relating that to the number of people able to undertake this amount of work; with costs albeit often demanding a compromise.

Secondly, sales must be fitted into the organization structure. This too is dependent on size and activity. Questions such as: how many sales people can one manager manage? How many different types of sales people are necessary? How many territories or groups of customer have to be serviced? It may be that a sales director heads up the function and is supported by a sales manager with a number of area or regional managers reporting to them before the sales people appear. It may be, in a small organization, that the general manager must cope with all of this. Two factors should primarily be born in mind.

» *Customer categories*: for example, in the way that a building materials company might need to relate to: building firms and contractors (large and small), architects, surveyors, builders' merchants, local authorities, government departments and maybe more. In this case they might have different people calling on specifiers (architects and others) and direct purchasers. The complexities here will dictate the scale and arrangement of the organization structure.

» *Number of customers*: obviously if the customer base is small less sales people are needed to cover them and vice versa. Similarly if part of the job of selling is done in some way separate from a field sales operation: online or on the telephone, for instance.

Key issues

In considering organization, remember:

» *to review regularly*: it is a variable. Many organizations hit problems because their sales organization becomes regarded as fixed, and then – over time – ceases to match the market conditions. External changes can accelerate this;

» *to link with marketing*: sometimes marketing innovation necessitates change. For example, Usborne who sell books for children use normal channels and sales organization, selling to book shops etc. They also sell through party style events (like Tupperware) getting mothers with small children to organize gatherings at their homes to demonstrate and sell books. This works well, but represents a change that needs different people and organization to make this side of their operation work; and

» *to prompt organization at individual territory level*: the way individual sales people manage their own "patch" is also vital. They need to link intentions for call frequency and the customer mix (large and small) to a map and ensure that the way they "work" the territory is efficient and productive (e.g. minimizing travel time and cost). Again this is something they need to be reminded to review regularly.

STAFFING

One of the key issues addressed in the final chapter (Chapter 10) is staffing. The rule here is simply stated. Assemble and maintain a team of good people. There is no room for passengers, and poor performers can end up monopolizing a sales manager's time and this, in turn causes other problems as other things are delayed or neglected.

Recruitment must be thorough and systematic. A systematic approach is recommended by many authorities. The following eight-stage approach is the basis of comment on this subject by Mike Wilson in his book *Managing a Sales Force*.

1 *Writing a job description*: this is worth spending some time on. It should spell out the tasks in full (it is not enough just to say it is "*to sell the product*"). If prospecting is necessary say so. If a successful candidate must be able to give a technical demonstration of the product, work at the bottom of a mine shaft or carry out the sale in five minutes while the buyer mans a busy cash till in a store of some sort, say so. Beyond duties and tasks this document can record such matters as reporting lines, evaluation procedures, and remuneration.

2 *Writing a profile of the person*: what kind of person is likely to be successful in the job? List basic characteristics (e.g. age, experience), character (e.g. persistent, self-reliant), motivations (e.g. attitudes to money, security etc.), emotional maturity (e.g. profile, capacity for self-discipline etc.). Past experience and what successes it has

brought them are important here; so too are details (more than one sales person has been appointed before it was discovered they could not drive a car!).

3 *Recruiting candidates*: review the options. You can advertise (in local or national papers, trade magazines etc.), but do not overlook other channels such as looking internally or asking existing staff for recommendations (and paying a reward if successful candidates are produced this way). If you use an agency it may seem expensive – but so is your time! And try to get a personal recommendation, there are agencies and agencies (and currently a look on the Internet identifies more than 5000 agencies operating that way; take care – some will not be there tomorrow).

4 *Assessing application forms*: a good application form (which these days might be completed on line) is invaluable. Ask for comprehensive information, match it to the job description and profile and plan to interview *only* those who show well at this stage. The whole process works better with more forms and less interviews rather than the reverse.

5 *Checking references*: not always easy, but worth doing (telephoning those a candidate gives permission to contact may be best) – and worth doing up front. If it shows up any "nasties" then you save the time of the other stages.

6 *Testing*: similarly this is better done before interviewing. Some things are clear: you can test someone's fluency in French, numeracy or other straightforward skills precisely – and reject them if they are inadequate. Other tests need more care, though some swear by psychometric tests that profile candidates, they need careful choosing, add time and cost – and *none* can measure sales ability as a specific factor.

7 *Structured interviewing*: this stage links your details of the job and the candidate with their personal showing. It is worth cross-checking what was said on an application form (there is a considerable temptation to lie on them) – indeed the form can provide the structure for the interview. One main interview, and perhaps a shorter second one for a shortlist works well; a second opinion might be obtained from a colleague on the second one.

8 *Evaluating a shortlist and making a final decision*: Check the *facts*, relate one candidate to another objectively – trust your judgment and experience – but beware of irrational hunches and pseudo-psychology.

This is a pivotal task and needs special care and attention.

Key issues

» *Assumptions*: avoid making them. It is a common failing that people (especially men) believe they are a good, and worse, instant, judge of character – "*I know the good candidates within five minutes of beginning the interview.*" Research does not bear this out. Recruitment needs a systematic approach to be successful – you skimp this process at your peril.

» *Stereotypes*: avoid using descriptions of sales jobs that are totally cliché – if you say nothing in an advertisement other than asking for someone – "*dynamic, self-starting, highly motivated, persistent, personable and of exceptional character*" – most people reading it will say – "*That's me.*" Be factual about the job.

» *Local difficulty*: as has been made clear, this is not an area for compromise. Bad selection leads, almost inevitably, to bad performance and you very rarely hear sales managers say that someone turned out better than they thought at interview stage. So if there is a particular problem (e.g. the difficulty of full employment in somewhere like Singapore) it must not be allowed to weaken resolve to make the right appointment.

» *Legislation*: make sure that all records, forms, contracts and processes are as they should be (check with your HR [human resources] department). In an increasingly litigious world you do not want to run foul of the law when candidates are rejected or unsuccessful people have contracts terminated.

» *Experiment*: and do not be hidebound by convention. For example, why do all prospective candidates have to have a degree, or have ten years experience in your industry? Maybe the place to fish is in new pools – in your own factory or amongst groups less obviously qualified.

DEVELOPING

This is, without doubt, the most important element of the sales manager's job. It starts as people are recruited.

» *Induction training*: even if you recruit experienced sales people they need how to operate in your environment. They need to know about your organization and product, they need to understand the kind of people who will be their customers, and they need to know how – exactly how – selling skills can be appropriately and effectively deployed for you. Time spent at this stage can pay dividends. Some things can be delegated, but beware. You do not want technical product knowledge put over by someone with no understanding of customers, and much – maybe most – of what must be done is best done by the manager.

» *Field training*: time must be spent regularly in the field, joint calling, with people – including experienced people. Selling is dynamic and needs constant fine-tuning. A cycle of evaluation, counseling and action and advice to focus the sales person's thinking on the quality of their approach and back to evaluation is a continuous process.

» The most important objective here relates to the numbers involved. Working *with the sales person* (this is not, and must not be seen as, checking, control, or instruction) on a small, but regular and representative number of calls is a means of making all the many others they make alone go well.

» *The most important aspect of the role is to establish the habit of self-evaluation and fine-tuning in people, making them better able to operate alone and making it more likely that they will always do so at the peak of performance.*

» It is beyond the scope of this work to recommend specific evaluation systems on which to base this sort of process, but some formality of system may help. It must be tailor-made and seen to be clear, constructive, consistent, and fair – and above all practical, it must actually help review and improve performance.

» *Group activities*: field training allows the identification of common needs for development, which can then be better addressed on a group basis; one of the key reasons for having sales meetings. These must be well planned and conducted, constructive in manner, content and approach – and must make a difference. Poor meetings quickly dilute motivation. Development activities here can involve people in, for example, leading projects and also allow other methods to be used such as role-playing, training exercises or training films.

» *Formal training*: sometimes development needs more formal solution. In a larger organization help may come from an HR department or there may be a training resource center (with a library and facilities to view videos or undertake e-learning of various sorts). Sometimes the answer may be an external or internal course, the latter can be tailored; sometimes the manager may be able to conduct short sessions themselves, alternatively there may be value in having assistance from a consultant.

The ongoing need for development should never be underestimated; equally any development activity should be practically based and genuinely likely to help maintain or improve performance. At the end of the day the person most likely to be able to do this on a regular basis is the sales person themselves; but the manager should play a part and be an effective catalyst to more.

Key issues

As has been made clear the development task is probably the single most important thing sales managers can spend time on; indeed it must take up most of their time. A constructive view must always be taken of it, therefore, and thus the following need addressing.

» *Time*: in modern business, pressure on time seems to increase constantly. Managers must fight to spend an appropriate amount of time on this process. In a large organization different levels of sales management may help spread the load (regional and area managers, for instance). For others the key task is to balance overall workload – and sales managers seem inclined to have a wide range of responsibilities beyond actually managing the sales team (getting involved in everything from promotion to pricing). If sales approaches are to truly differentiate from competition, ways must be found to give this area priority.

» *The personal touch*: with more and more training provided through technology, and for sales people in isolation (e.g. computer based training), there is a danger that actual face to face contact declines. By all means use technology or anything else that helps, but the key activity of individuals working creatively together may achieve most and this effect must not be diluted.

» *Perception of the role*: the days of sales managers being regarded as primarily having a "police" role are, for the most part, long gone. Yet with control being part of the job, it is important that the relationship between sales people and their manager is, and is seen to be, constructive. Too often one hears sales people say something like "*I never seem to see my manager unless there is something wrong.*" Managers must work *with* people, not just be seen as checking up on them or telling them what to do. Learning – certainly that prompts consistently different future practice – will only take place if lessons are made acceptable and people are involved in the process. New ideas, and thus new methods and approaches, will only be sparked or evolved if people work constructively and creatively together (the airline industry example in Chapter 2 makes this point).

MOTIVATING

It is an inherent part of any manager's job to motivate. The motivational "climate," the net effect of many influences on people in their work, has a very real impact on the way they do their job. If development ensures that people are able to do what is required, then motivation ensures that they want to do so.

For sales people, faced with the attrition of customer attitudes, and often working largely on their own, the way they feel about their job is especially important. The theory of motivation that provides the most practical basis for a concept that links easily to action is that of Frederick Herzberg (see the section Key Concepts and Thinkers). His description of satisfiers and dissatisfiers, provides a good analogy for balancing motivational influences: actively creating positive feeling and acting also to minimize negative feelings. For example, most sales people hate administration, but it needs to be done. It may always be an essentially negative aspect of the job, however explaining why it is necessary and creating the minimum straightforward system to get it done is appreciated, and that aspect becomes motivational.

Incentives are perhaps worth a special word. Research over the years seems to show consistently that the best performing sales people have a reward system that includes some element of payment on results. This is not always possible. Results need to be readily linked to individual effort (team incentives are less powerful). Such schemes need to be straightforward (it is no good if an hour needs to be spent with a calculator just to see how things are going); they must pay out regularly (for some sales people thinking about Friday-week is long-term planning); they must represent a significant proportion of total remuneration (and that means bearing in mind family income); and they should be interesting – fun – linking to published results, newsletters, and league tables all help.

Variety is important too. Incentives can be linked to all sorts of things, overall sales but also opening new accounts, selling in a new product or profitability of sales. Simple quarterly schemes, with regular changes work well, as do mixing financial reward with other incentives (travel is a favorite). But a simple *"Well done"* can be as powerful as anything – and costs nothing. Motivation is a key part of sales management and managers who are, or make themselves, instinctive motivators have a real asset in their management armory.

Key issues

» *Time pressure*: without a doubt low motivation is more often a result of less being done than should be, than of the wrong thing being done. Motivating does take time, but it is time well spent – it needs building in as a priority.

» *Resisting magic formulae*: the easiest trap to fall into is a belief that money is a panacea. Incentives, including financial incentives, have a role to play. But a mix of activities is best, and small influences are just as important in the total picture as large. To motivate successfully you must work at it; the effort is worthwhile, the process can quickly become a habit and it can be as pleasurable to motivate as to be motivated.

» *Being censorious*: what matters most is the people. It is easy to base motivational practice on what *you* would like, when sales people may have different priorities.
» *Caring*: if there is anything like a magic formula in this area, then it is that the simpler things – just taking an interest in people, working constructively with them, giving them authority, and recognizing achievements are probably more important than anything. But they have to be *real*. The manager needs to care (and the old saying that – *"if you can fake the sincerity, everything else is easy"* – must *never* be allowed to become the basis for action).

CONTROL

The word control can have connotations of "policing." In fact the concept is simple and constructive; it revolves around the following equation:

$$A - S = \pm V$$

Actual performance (A) is compared with a preset standard (S) and action is considered, and if necessary taken, by considering the variance (V) between the two.

A variety of standards can be used and these may relate to everything from the number of calls made in a day to the sales of a particular product. In nature they are:

» *absolute standards*: these are specific targets (e.g. annual sales revenue). They are important, but only provide certain information;
» *moving standards*: these look at results over time (e.g. a moving annual total) and thus highlight more about trends and likely outcome; and
» *diagnostic standards*: as the name suggests these are designed to show the reasons why results are as they are.

In selling there are only four key variables: who is called on (the nature and type of customer or prospect); how many people are called on (more potential customers seen = potentially more sales); how often they are called on (call frequency); and – a whole separate area – what is done face to face with the customer (the quality and effectiveness of the sales approach).

The essence of control is change. The knowledge of what is happening allows action to be taken either aiming to bring things back on track if there is a shortfall, or to build on success. This last point is key. Control is not simply to correct faults. It is to accentuate the positive. It is just as useful to see a positive variance, ask why this should be happening and build on the action that is creating it. While management has a duty to provide a framework and encourage discipline amongst sales people, their prime job is to act as a catalyst to success. By viewing control as both focusing on positive and negative results and acting as a spur to change, its value will be maximized.

Key issues

» *A surfeit of information*: the biggest problem these days may seem perverse. There is too much information. Certainly information is probably easier to collect and more up to date than was the case in the past, but key indicators can get buried. Management must focus on those factors (whatever they are from volume of sales to the number of new accounts opened) that are key; and must know what they are.

» *Optimizing information collection*: however information is collected, and it may be filling in a form or inputting to a computer of some sort, the process must not be over-engineered. Making sales people aware of how important it is, and making the system straightforward should get information flowing well; this must not be an area of constant hassle as this just wastes time and puts the veracity of information in doubt

» *Fit internal aspects of control to the outside world*: for example, if sales people man an exhibition stand at a trade show at the beginning of the financial year, high sales volume over this time may negate the effect of incentive schemes throughout the remainder of the year.

LOOKING AHEAD

It has been mentioned several times in this work that selling is a dynamic process. One of any sales manager's key tasks is to ensure their team is selling in just the right way. Indeed their job takes its shape from that of those they manage. So it is a prerequisite that they are not only able to define what is necessary *now*, but that they are ahead of the game in spotting, better still predicting, changes that will require changes to sales practice. None of us can be sure what the future holds; however working to keep ahead can be approached systematically. The following questions flag the areas that need watching:

» what further changes will technology bring?
» how will the sales function fit in future within the organization's total marketing mix?
» with whom precisely will responsibility for individual customers (especially large ones) lie?
» how is the role of the sales force changing?
» what range of tasks will the members of the sales team need to perform in future?
» what skills – and new or changed skills – will they need to have at their command?
» what new pressures will competition bring to bear and how will that change what we need to do?
» how do we rate against competitors and on the broader stage (including international competition and market activity)? and
» what different expectations will customers have in future and what new demands will they make?

SUMMARY

Overall, sales managers have a multifaceted task. Each aspect of it is important. Some responsibilities are more occasional than others. For example, time spent on recruitment must be well organized and wisely spent, but it is not something that must be done every day (well, not in a good sales organization!). Conversely, time spent on a variety of counseling and development tasks are literally day by day tasks.

Key to being a successful sales manager is *getting the balance right*; and being equally effective in a disparate list of operational areas.

The preceding section focused primarily on tasks, finally the following sets out a check list more in terms of the personal characteristics of the successful sales manager, who must:

» have *knowledge of marketing* and an involvement in it, because sales is an inherent part of the marketing mix;

» be an *effective manager*, able to direct, control and inspire a team of usually free-spirited people;

» take the *long view* (directing activities, setting strategic objectives and defining a framework of targets, policies and priorities to drive towards them);

» be a *corporate team player*, as liaison with many different parts of the business is mandatory and must be done effectively;

» be *productive* – able to balance conflicting priorities and still spend sufficient time with the team, singly and as a group; this is something that demands problem solving and decision-making abilities;

» *sell effectively*. They do not need to be the best on the team, but must understand and be able to practice the full gambit of techniques involved: sales, negotiation, presentation, numeracy etc.;

» stay *close to the market*, because achieving a customer focus in sales activities is always key;

» c*ommunicate effectively* – with staff, colleagues and customers; and

» a*chieve results*. Managing the activity is not enough – it must work.

Perhaps in one way or another everything here comes back to customers. In the survey *The Future of Selling* (see Chapter 8) the future role is defined as follows:

> "Tomorrow's sales leaders will need to develop a clear view of the way ahead for the customers in their industries, and be able to provide their sales people with the direction and competencies to take full advantage of the opportunities available."

In Practice

How can day to day sales management be made to work? Chapter 7 looks at cases and ideas to see how a practical and creative approach can help.

"Information's pretty thin stuff, unless mixed with experience."
Clarence Day, American essayist

In this section, the principal tasks identified in Chapter 6, are exemplified by comment about how sales managers are currently operating and what makes for success. The intention here is not to focus on major strategies, still less to suggest one ideal way of operating. Rather it is to highlight approaches and thinking that is useful, and show how the right approach can help whether applied to major or, seemingly, minor matters.

CASE 1

This appears simple, but is a clear and positive example of management providing support that changes selling practice, that is realistically linked to practical issues about how the customer buys.

One segment of the market of an international hotel group was for their conference business – the use of meeting rooms for everything from training seminars to wedding receptions.

The situation

The sales team aimed at, and succeeded in, meeting most prospective buyers at their properties. The hotel itself was their most valuable visual aid. A tour of the hotel was a core part of their exchange with customers, and clearly an inspection of the meeting rooms was an important part of the proceedings for conference customers.

The sales staff were clearly experienced regarding the use of their own property. They were well able to offer good advice of which rooms to use for what. But, most often, of course, they were showing people around when rooms were empty. An empty conference room is not at its most impressive, particularly if it stores stacks of tables, chairs and other items ready for the next event. While staff were well informed and enthusiastic, just saying, *"This is what I would recommend for your (wedding reception or whatever)"* left a great deal to the imagination of the customer. Discussing a wedding, for example, a sales person could stand in the recommended room and *see* clearly in their mind's eye how it would be – the flowers, the sparkling glasses, the crisp white tablecloths and smiling guests. They *knew* such an occasion would be memorable.

But the customer just saw an empty room, and too many of them headed off to inspect somewhere else. Sometimes coincidence meant that they could be shown an event in full swing. Sometimes they could be asked back during a similar event, but they had to be made to feel it was worthwhile to do so.

The action

Imagination is always assisted by *seeing* something. The job was not to *show them the room*. Rather it was *to make them believe their function would go well there and help them imagine it doing just that*. The sales manager commissioned a portfolio of high quality photographs, and put them into a presentation folder that the sales people could go through with prospective customers. If they needed a business meeting then business meetings could be shown, workshops, conferences – a range of meetings, laid out in different ways and photographed (with the permission of past users) to show how well they suited people. For a wedding the flowers and everything else was there – clear, colorful and promising similar satisfaction to the next happy couple; and so on.

The organization of this, which went way beyond the shots in brochures (mainly empty of people), took a little time and cost some money. The usefulness of the material was self-apparent and, after just a short briefing, the results in use were tangible:

» sales increased;
» bookings made on a first visit increased;
» sales people had more confidence (and their motivation was positively affected);
» the sales approach was easier to personalize (an important factor – being taken robot-like on what seems to be the same tour as everyone else does not impress prospects who, like all customers, want to be treated like individuals); and
» customers liked it and commented on it (in terms of it adding to the service they were receiving).

In a service business such an initiative is clearly especially important. Sales aids are often important in many industries. The job of the sales manager is not just to chase people to use what is there (perhaps what has always been there!). It is to think about what will help, and provide everything possible – with an eye on both sales people and customers. As this example shows such ideas need not be complicated or costly, but they can certainly help boost sales.

CASE 2: DOTTING THE "I"S

The following example, paraphrasing the experience of an international financial services firm, shows the importance of getting the real facts, and of attention to detail.

The sales people were involved in a classic long-term cycle in getting business. It ran from making initial contact to a meeting, a written proposal, follow up action and sometimes further meetings with formal presentations also being necessary on occasions. The success rate of each stage was closely monitored, so that management knew how many initial contacts were necessary, on average, to produce a set number of meetings – indeed all the ratios of this sort were monitored. On the success of written proposals moving things to the next stage the ratio seemed low, especially where large projects were involved.

This was bad enough, but of course anything that failed to move on at this stage had taken up a fair amount of time, effort and therefore money – all of which had to be duplicated to produce a replacement prospect.

Research was conducted (formal research handled by a consultant) to ascertain how prospects viewed the quality and nature of the written proposals. This was relatively quick and easy to do as it was addressed to major recent prospects (who had declined to take things further). It showed that proposals were viewed as being different from prior discussions (which had been rated highly), as one respondent said "*almost as if they had come from different people.*" The detail was analyzed (too long, over-formal, unclear, impersonal) and training organized to address the specific differences in writing approach that prospects found desirable.

Over a comparatively short period of time, as new – and better crafted – proposals went out the ratio of success climbed positively and significantly. The moral is clear: analysis of the sales job, real information about customer expectations, and action to get the detail right pays off. Two caveats: as customer expectations, likes, and dislikes etc. change nothing must be left unreviewed for ever on the assumption that it is now satisfactory. One aspect here was the effective tailoring of material to individual prospects – in other words, as with so much else in selling, a standardized approach risks alienating people.

CASE 3

Given the importance of training, both formal and informal, to sales management in maximizing the effectiveness of the sales team, one case here should surely touch on this topic. There are numbers of problems here, for example to:

» provide induction training that gets people off to a good start, providing a basis for their future sales activity and helping develop good habits (not least the habit of acting on the need for self evaluation and fine-tuning of sales approaches);
» allocate sufficient time to field evaluation and development and maintain that consistently in the face of other pressures; and
» ring the changes, so that attention and time are focused again on key issues which might otherwise cease to be thought about, with people lapsing into an unthinking "automatic pilot" approach that fails to achieve the best possible performance.

The latter example above can be approached in many ways with the same topic being investigated through exercises, role-playing, films, projects and more – with each exposure adding to people's awareness in a fresh way.

Even so, such a chain of differing approaches needs creative thought. New ideas are required, ideally of course combining novelty with practicality. The following certainly does that and, although originated by a trade body, illustrates the kind of thinking that any organization can apply.

The UK Meetings Industry Association has a membership primarily representing operators of hotel and conference venues. In many ways, including sales, this is a specialist area of business. Certainly it is one where an exclusivity is felt, thus the utilization of sales training in generic form is lower than in some industries. The education committee resolved to create something specific to assist member organizations.

The suggestion of making a film was promptly rejected. Too expensive, it was thought – a thought that many individual organizations have had. However, on reflection, a way was found. The film was to be low cost and focus on defined aspects of sales technique. Costs were kept down because, unusually, the film was shot live and the characters filmed were real. A venue was found who agreed to host the exercise, a sales situation was identified involving one of the sales team from a member company and a real client. Their permission and co-operation were obtained, and with some briefing a real meeting was filmed literally as it happened. With minimal editing, and some added commentary (and an accompanying workbook) it became as useful as many a more professionally made film – and had the merit of reflecting the exact situation of the kind of business involved.

The training input here *was* important (the author was involved as consultant), but so was the industry input. The main point here is that the format itself was the novelty that allowed something different to be created; something of considerable training value. Any organization could do something similar, even if a little professional assistance was needed it is a low cost option, yet provides something tailor made for what sales management must do.

HORSES FOR COURSES

Here are a few examples of practice that is designed to maximize effectiveness by reflecting the special nature of the fields in which sales people work.

» In selling *pharmaceutical products* sales people selling direct to doctors, either general practitioners or in hospitals, have only a limited time to sell; GPs are reported to allow an average of four minutes to someone detailing, as it is called, their products. Much effort goes into both defining what can usefully done in such a time (clearly it must be focused) and into practicing succinct yet persuasive call content that can get a worthwhile message over fast.

Other methods are also used to get round the problem, for example presentations to a number of doctors at a group practice.

» In selling *agricultural products* sales people find that farmers, as well as expecting them to be knowledgeable about their products and applications (in what conditions precisely is a particular weed killer suitable?), want them to be participative. A pair of wellington boots in the car is a prime piece of equipment, and many a new recruit has been taken the muddy route (or worse!) to inspect a field by a farmer regarding them as "wet behind the ears."

» In selling in *financial markets* the old ways of 9–5 working hours have long gone. Customers may work long, or odd hours – to tie in with the working hours of an overseas stock exchange perhaps – and expect their suppliers to do the same.

It may seem basic, but such practices are not universally followed. By matching to the realities of markets and customers, sales people can increase the chances of a fair reception. Such factors change and thus need keeping an eye on – more evidence of the dynamic nature of sales. This is another area to look at to create differentiation.

A GOOD IDEA

Finally, in this chapter, it is worth noting that sales management is made more effective in all sorts of ways if approaches are well thought out. Seemingly simple ideas can have a considerable effect.

» *Timesaving administration*: sales people are not renowned for their love of administration. One idea, used now by many companies, provides an appropriate incentive to get the administrative tasks done, done right and done on time. Usually on a monthly basis sales people have to complete and return a number of reports (from call reports to competitive intelligence). These may be of no central use until everything is in and can be consolidated, and – if one is late – it sparks off a series of time wasting "chasers." The answer? To have a mandatory rule: anyone whose required reports are not in on time, complete and legible (a good many are still on paper) has their expenses claim payment delayed until the next month. It works. It is seen as fair (if explained) and, in terms of management style, can be balanced by putting the chasing time saved to use with discursive approaches to things that matter more.

» *Spicing up sales meetings*: it is a useful measure of sales management competence to ask a member of a sales team, "*What was your last sales meeting like?*" If they groan then there should probably be some changes. A key rule is to ensure that there is sufficient participation. As well as just asking questions and involving people in discussion more may be necessary. One sales manager (now forgotten) showed me a brief checklist they had developed of all the elements that could be added. They always utilized one – or more – and rang the changes to ensure variety. The elements were: role-play; demonstration; brainstorming; games, quizzes, tests or competitions; exercises (practicing or experimenting with something); formal presentations; analysis (e.g. to produce an action plan for a major customer); films (linked to discussion or exercise); awards; debate or visitors (from another department or even a customer, though perhaps in some cases the visit should not last throughout the whole meeting).

» *Heavy traffic*: given the increasingly slow speed of traffic in most major cities, sales people the world over spend more and more of their time traveling – time spent in the car that is essentially non-productive. There may be comparatively little that can be done about this, though:

  » some companies have banned sales people from moving around in core city centers. They expect to see a receipt for parking the car and sales people walking from one central contact to another;

  » more and more organizations use audio tape for communication (e.g. to update product information) which can be played while driving; and

  » at the same time, mobile telephones can be useful, but can also be dangerous (more companies now lay down rules for this area – and perhaps more need to do so).

» *Delegation*: all sales managers experience the need for what are usually called PR (public relations) calls – when customers say, in whatever way, "*I must see the manager.*" Sometimes this is necessary and useful but, while managers need to do some selling (or they may get out of touch), such calls can prove unnecessary and reduce time that should be spent on management tasks. One resolution managers might make is at least to query these requests. It is easy to be flattered and feel that no one else can deal with it – but these are prime opportunities to delegate. For example, managers can:

» make such calls joint calls, involving one of the team;
» use this to make sure that customers see the team as their prime contact; or
» simply brief a sales person and delegate the call, explaining to the customer, indeed making a virtue of the change. This combines development to extend skills with added responsibilities for coping with a wider range of customers and situations.

» *Major customer strategies*: the fact that a customer is large can, perhaps perversely, mean that less planning takes place – a large order becomes routine and seems to negate the need to check that the full potential is being exploited. To combat this, draw attention to the need and get and keep activity moving; one sales manager set up regular lunch meetings. With the inducement of free sandwiches, he got people together in small groups that met regularly; each meeting focused on one major customer and debated the best action for say the next three months of operations. In this way each sales person had to review some of their major customers – and got the benefit of others' advice in so doing. The meetings were enjoyed, put good ideas on the table and led to positive action and recognizably additional sales.

» *No such thing*! Just to show that even the smallest thing can bring change and improvement, I would note that *banning*, with attendant fuss, the use of that ubiquitous piece of sales jargon "the courtesy call" from all call reports (where it so often appears instead of anything more descriptive) can produce better planned, more effective calls and improve sales. *All* calls need objectives. Just calling in to say "*Hi*" or because the customer is always good for a cup of decent tea is not enough!

QUOTE

In one American publishing company the sales manager is quoted as saying that they had found the perfect incentive scheme – "*every month we fire the guy at the bottom of the sales league*! "

Key Concepts and Thinkers

Chapter 8 adds a glossary of key terminology and investigates ideas and concepts that can make the process of sales management easier and more certain to succeed.

» Glossary
» The sales profile
» Customer orientation
» Sales productivity
» Customer organization
» Customer profitability
» Customer relationships
» Key thinkers

"If there's one constant about customers, it's that they will change – in taste, in attitude, and in demands. So we will continue to learn. Continue to think like a customer and find new ways to give them the best possible experience."

Charlie Bell, CEO of McDonalds in Australia

There is not a great deal of dedicated terminology in the specific area of sales management (though it shares much general management jargon). However, the following can be noted.

GLOSSARY

Kerbside conference – the post call "post-mortem" and development session held when a manager is accompanying sales people in the field (which may often take place in the car – hence the name).

Key/major/national accounts – a variety of names are used here. First, measures vary as to what a major customer is, simplistically it is only what an individual organization finds significant. A second significant factor is the lead time involved. In industries selling, say, capital equipment it may take many months from first meeting to contract and there is an overlap here with "major sales."

Award scheme – an incentive scheme based on non-financial rewards (such as merchandising or travel); beware – such schemes need to be carefully checked for tax implications, it is not motivational for a sales person to return from a wonderful holiday to an unexpected tax bill.

Call frequency – the number of times in a year a customer is scheduled to receive regular calls; sometimes used to categorize customers and describe their relative importance.

Call plan – the statement of work to be done with customers, arranged with productivity and effectiveness in mind.

Competitor intelligence – the information collected about competitive products and services and their suppliers that may specifically be used to improve the approach taken on a call.

Contract sales force – this refers to freelance or agency-provided sales staff who are not employed by those for whom they sell. Such teams may be used on a permanent basis or over a short period (to boost sales in a seasonal business or launch a new product, perhaps linked to a test market).

Ego Drive/Empathy – Mayer and Goldberg's terms for, respectively: the internal motivational drive that makes the good sales person *want* to succeed, and the ability to see things from other peoples' (customers) point of view – and, importantly, being seen to do so.

Field training – simply training, or development, activity away from any formal setting, undertaken out and about on territory.

Incentive/commission – whatever the dictionary may say, the way these words need interpreting in sales is as follows: *Commission* rewards past performance. *Incentives* prompt better performance (and the addressing of particular targets) for the future. Thus commission may not act as an incentive, and incentives may involve much more than the financial payments that usually comprise commission.

On-the-job training – field training and development activity.

Pie system – a structured way of managing the spread of customers and prospects around a sales territory.

Petal system – a practical way of organizing journeys to minimize time and mileage and thus help maximize productivity.

Remuneration – a general term, which with sales people implies the inclusion of elements of their reward package that are specific to the sales job: car, incentives etc.

Sales audit – an, occasional, systematic review of all aspects of the sales activity and its management to identify areas needing improvement, or working well and needing extension; a process that recognizes the inherent dynamic nature of sales.

Sales productivity – the sales equivalent of productivity in an area, the focus here is on efficiencies that maximize the amount of time spent with customers (rather than traveling, writing reports etc.): it focuses on ratios and touches on anything that increases sales success however measured.

SPIN – although this is a registered trademark, it is heard used generically – spin – to describe a customer focused and questioning based approach to identifying needs and selling appropriately in light of this knowledge.

Standards – preset targets (absolute, moving or diagnostic standards are all used). This is reviewed in Chapter 6 "The State of the Art – Control".

Territory – the area covered by an individual sales person. It is usually, but not always, geographic.

In addition, there is terminology used by sales people and about selling. There is too much to list comprehensively here, the following simply provides some examples:

Benefits – reasons to buy, specifically what a product or service does for or means to a buyer (as distinct from features, factual aspects about a product). Used in various ways, e.g. benefit selling.

Cold calling – approaches to potential customers by any method (face to face or telephone, say) who are "cold" – have expressed no prior interest of any sort.

Gatekeeper – someone who through their position can facilitate or deny access to a buyer (e.g. a secretary).

Influencers – people who, while not having exclusive authority to buy, influence the buyer, through their recommendation.

Qualifying prospects – research or action to produce information to demonstrate that cold prospects are "warm."

KEY CONCEPTS

Sales management is a personal – people to people – task. Its successful practice lies not so much in the adoption of key concepts (unless the conviction that sales people *need* managing is one such), rather in the systematic and thorough addressing of the key tasks of sales management reviewed at some length in Chapters 6 and 10.

Certain more conceptual factors are, however, worth keeping in mind.

The sales profile

Selling, and sales management along with it, have never been viewed in quite the same way as other, perhaps sexier, marketing techniques. Selling suffers from a low status image virtually worldwide, perhaps only in the United States is this less so. Externally there is a classic suspicion of "someone with something to sell," even internally there can be a "them and us" situation of some friction, with inside people perhaps not understanding what sales people who are out of the office all day actually do.

Action: sales management has a key task to create a belief, at least in their own organization, that selling (and managing selling) is important and further that it deserves acknowledgement and should be accorded a high status. Management must also fight the sales peoples' corner on a day to day basis, and be seen to do so. If this is done and sales people themselves are made to believe that they are sincerely valued and respected, then the scene is set for them to succeed.

Customer orientation

Selling is well defined (by a character in a Video Arts training film) as *"helping people to buy."* Exactly so. Selling is not something to be done to people and everything about it and the way it is approached should reflect that fact.

The jargon of selling is rife with terms reflecting this: "benefit selling" has become a generic term emphasizing the need to discover what people want and *why* and sell accordingly. Other phrases have enjoyed some favor and emphasized the same point, for example "conceptual selling," meaning much the same or "strategic selling" which seems more vague and, anyway, would you sell unstrategically?

Action: to instill in sales people the concept of "customer first," not just as an obvious service view, but as a basis for the style of sales technique adopted.

Sales productivity

This is the concept of analysis and action to "squeeze a quart out of a pint pot." It focuses on the ratios involved (for example, the number of calls made/orders taken) and examines the whole sales process to see how much more can be got from the activity and to ensure that the *way* things are being undertaken is correctly based.

Action: this is an area for ongoing management checking and, if possible, innovation. The productivity of every aspect of the activity should be borne in mind, for example:

» documentation might be streamlined (or made electronic) to save time;

» territories and journey planning investigated to ensure it maximizes time spent with customers; and

» sales technique structured to be productive as well as effective (perhaps aiming for meetings that are shorter in duration, providing this is still effective and acceptable to customers).

Customer categorization

Customers are not all the same. The major way in which this is recognized is in terms of size. Big customers are not just larger, they are different in the way they must be dealt with to make the relationship work for both parties. However this is addressed, and it may need to juggle size, potential, location, industry or type, use of product, level of technicality ... and more, every customer must be provided with the right service and the right sales resource and approach.

Action: this is a dynamic area, managers and sales people alike need to focus on how this categorization is arranged and adapt regularly, constantly almost, so that every category is related within the best possible way.

Customer profitability

This has come to be more important as customers have polarized and the big have got bigger. As customer demands, or services offered (or both) extend, more and more margin is vulnerable to being eaten up in just getting the business.

Any company that analyses the costs of obtaining business may be shocked at just how many things seemingly conspire to reduce margin. These include: all the costs of the sales force (from recruitment to commission); discounts (and there may be many a different basis for them, e.g. quantity bought or when purchase is made); special packing, delivery (maybe to multiple locations, labeling; credit terms (and beyond), advertising and promotional support, merchandising assistance, training of customers' staff ... the list goes on. Unless this is addressed carefully profitability may well be in danger.

Action: management must address the list of possible "profit diluters," the policy involved and sales staffs' attitudes and competence. For example, it may be that policy is at fault and profit being lost because published terms need attention, or that policy is right, but that sales people are losing out due to poor negotiating skills.

Customer relationship

Every customer and supplier by definition presupposes a relationship. A variety of factors, not least the polarization of customer size (see above) have highlighted this and moved it from something that was taken for granted to something that should be planned. The electronic revolution has locked into this area, see Chapter 4 The E-Dimension, and for many the term CRM is synonymous with electronic records and prompt systems. As with so much else the key here is clear – it is the customer. Relationships need to reflect customer requirements and have as much in common with service as sales.

Action: the manager must make clear what is being aimed at here. Of course, the personal rapport between buyer and seller (sales person) is important here. But buyers do not now buy (if they ever did) just because they like people. They do buy, when their requirements are met by several potential suppliers, from the one who they feel goes about the process in the most acceptable and useful (and perhaps even the nicest) way.

KEY THINKERS

Management gurus abound. It is perhaps a reflection of the comments above about the profile of sales that, although there is plenty written about selling, albeit some of it in a much more evangelical style than is used for the discussion of other business skills, there have been few major sales management gurus.

The following, however, are worth mentioning.

Sales management

Frederick Herzberg

One task relates very specifically to the work of one man, the American psychologist Frederick Herzberg, who it is not an exaggeration to describe as the father of *motivational theory*. His views of how motivation works also make a very practical foundation to creating positive motivation and making it work.

Briefly, he described two categories of factor affecting peoples' motivation: first, *the dissatisfiers (or hygiene factors)* listed as:

» Company policy and administration
» Supervision
» Working conditions
» Salary
» Relationships with peers
» Personal life (and the impact of work on it)
» Status
» Security.

All these are external factors. When things suit in these areas – all will be well motivationally. If there are problems here (e.g. sales people feel they are being asked to complete endless, bureaucratic forms and reports for which they see no purpose), then positive motivation is quickly diluted. Secondly, *the satisfiers (or motivators)* that act to create positive motivation. These are more personal and can be listed as:

» Achievement
» Recognition
» The work itself
» Responsibility
» Advancement
» Growth.

A good analogy here is a glasshouse, and a phrase that is often used in this context is *motivational climate.* Just as the plants in a greenhouse can be influenced by many factors that affect temperature, opening doors or windows, painting the glass to reflect the sun, turning on the heater, so motivation can be influenced in many different ways.

The balance of factors is what matters. Managers should never underestimate the time and effort involved in getting things right here. Motivating is a continuous, time consuming process and attention to detail is vital. It is, however, very valuable, a well-motivated team will always focus better on the job and perform better as a result. It is a topic worth more study.

Herzberg's own books are now rather old and perhaps do not make good, practical references in the modern world. The workings of his theories and ideas on motivating successfully are explored in my own book *How to Motivate People* (Kogan Page/*The Sunday Times*).

Dartnell

The *Dartnell Salesmanagers Handbook* was the earliest reference of any substance on the subject. Today the Dartnell Corporation still occupies the role of sales management guru. Probably best known for their surveys – one of which looks at trends in training methods – their *Sales Force Compensation Survey* is an annual publication that is the prime reference in its area; the figures may apply to the USA, but many people would find the commentary and conclusions are worth a look.

Sales

Many early exponents are now no longer the benchmark for sales excellence, though it is worth recalling people such as Heinz Gold-mann whose sales and sales management seminars pulled hundreds of delegates over many years. His book *Winning Sales* is still worth reading, and shows the perennial nature of much to do with selling. Some, like Richard Denny who runs Leadership Development now operate in similar ways (his book, *Selling to Win, Kogan Page*, has a very personal style), but the most influential forces are rather different in nature.

Huthwaite Research Group

Without doubt one organization has added a whole new dimension to the way sales and selling are viewed, and thus to the practice of sales management, that is Huthwaite Research Group Limited. It is better known for its trademark, SPIN and the approach to selling this implies. Starting in the early seventies they applied new techniques to the observation of selling. Using behavior analysis, a research technique for observing and quantifying interactions between buyer and seller, it highlighted the interactive skills that seemed to best create successful sales. Key amongst them was questioning.

The main focus of their studies was on:

» how people buy and weigh up competitive offerings to help them make considered decisions;

» reactions, particularly negative ones, that buyers tend to have to being sold to;

» qualities that buyers regard as making a case (verbally or in writing) attractive, persuasive and credible; and

» the style of selling approach that appeared to be best regarded.

The fact that their views were based on, and validated by, research, literally thousands of interviews and observations of real sales meetings, was novel – they might say unique. In any case it was a key factor in helping make sales a profession. They offered training with sales techniques recommended by and matched to their studies, and their base of sales training has expanded to a full range of topics, including sales, negotiation, account management, major account strategies and sales management.

Though many would suggest that the Huthwaite research high-lighted, at least in part, approaches that were either common sense or which had been documented by others, their success in promoting their ideas certainly gave prominence to a very practical and logical way of looking at selling.

The key to the approach is customer focus. Once selling was regarded as something "you did to people," now it is predominantly seen as a process of helping and working with the psychological process by which people make decisions to buy. Key therefore is the concept of discovering, through very specifically applied questioning techniques (this is where the patented SPIN technique comes in), exactly what is happening on the customer's side of the discussion. If sales people find out about a customer, how they think, what they need, how they operate and what their expectations are of their suppliers and those that represent them, they will more precisely be able to focus their sales approach. The concept of the sales professional and of the sales person as advisor is also key to the approach. This may seem less than novel now, but everything about selling that builds in these kind of approaches (wherever they come from) tends to work best in the real world.

If selling is not, as is sometimes imagined, a matter that can be applied largely by rote – and it is not – then the implications for the sales manager are clear. Their job is not to lay down the law, setting out *the* way in which selling should take place. Rather it is to give sales people the understanding of the approach that must be taken, based on customer practice and expectations, and the confidence to do it in their own way – and in a way that is always tailored to individual customers.

Neil Rackham, of Huthwaite Research, has also written extensively. His books:

Making Major Sales
Account Strategy for Major Sales
The Management of Major Sales (written with Richard Ruff)
Getting Partnering Right
are all useful.

Other books

The practical nature of sales management means that there is a profusion of books, but your choice is very much a matter of taste as their content does not vary as much as their style and treatment. The following are chosen as a good cross section and to illustrate different options.

» *Sales Force Management*: Churchill, Ford, Walker, Johnston and Tanner: Irwin McGraw-Hill, sixth edition. This is the best of the major works on the subject, in more than 700 pages every conceivable aspect of sales management is touched on to some extent. It has cases and examples aplenty and links to a Website where there are exercises, cases, videos and PowerPoint presentations.

Link: www.mhhe.com/business/marketing/salesmanagement

» *Managing a Sales Force*: Michael T. Wilson: Gower Publishing. This is a practical workbook, referred to elsewhere, which is an excellent reference to all the essential tasks and how to undertake them. Prompted by this book, other titles came from the Marketing Improvements Group encapsulating their approach to some of the topics in more detail: these included – *Training Salesmen on the Job, Recruiting and Selecting Successful Salesmen* and *Motivating your Sales Force*. All are published by the same publisher.

» *Successful Sales Management*: Grant Stewart: Prentice Hall. A recent paperback that provides a clear review of all the basics. Its author, once a member of the Marketing Improvements team, draws on *Managing a Sales Force* above. The book was written when the author was a tutor on sales management at Ashridge Management College.

» *Sales Management*: Theory and Practice: B Donaldson: MacMillan Publishers.

Resources

If further investigation is necessary, this section will help. It sets out sources of reference looking at sales management in a number of different ways.

» Research
» Journals
» Using training films
» Professional bodies

"A little knowledge that acts is worth infinitely more than much knowledge that is idle."

Kahlil Gibran

What external resources can add power to the sales manager's arm? The following are necessarily a disparate group and no attempt is made to reduce them to neat categories. So, with books dealt with in the previous section "Concepts and Thinkers," listed here are sources of ideas, information and inspiration varying from films to professional institutes and web sites.

A key issue throughout this work has been the question of defining the sales job realistically and usefully. So we start with research.

RESEARCH

The Future of Selling is a report published late in 2000 by Quest Media Ltd (the publishers of the journal *Winning Business*) in association with the Institute of Professional Selling and consultants Miller Heinman Inc. This is an interesting research study, more so because the area is rarely researched. It reviews current practice and looks to the future examining: the changing sales role, customer expectations and beliefs, and the whole way sales teams are organized, staffed, rewarded and managed.

Key findings indicated that:

» customers are becoming better informed and more organized, demanding and sharp in their dealings with sales people (with the Internet being used to a significant extent for pre-buying research);
» technology is having, and will continue to have, an effect on sales activity: most dramatically it is replacing sales people with electronic, impersonal buying, though this is not affecting large numbers of business areas. The dynamic nature of this area is evidenced by the uncertainty respondents reflected in their forecasts of the other influences that are becoming important;
» recruitment is a perpetual challenge as is retention;
» CRM is becoming a more widespread basis for many customer interactions, and creating a more formal basis for them;

» training remains a constant need (and more of it is being done, and the range of ways in which it is done are also increasing) as the level of competency of sales people is seen as key to success; and

» reporting takes a high proportion of working time – reducing sales people's time spent face to face with customers; this despite the increasing computerization of data collection and reporting systems.

Sales management, its practice, manner and style, is seen as significant to success. On the one hand the increasing professionalism of the sales role, and the broadening of sales people's responsibilities in response to market changes, heighten the role and managerial skills sales managers must have. On the other hand, there is one area where sales managers seem sometimes to be marginalized. This is in respect of new technology. For example, sales managers are often not involved in the development of e-business strategies. There are dangers here. An e-business strategy that is not made compatible with traditional sales processes may lack realism. While technology and its development are always difficult to predict, it is perhaps best done in this area with the sales manager's active involvement, or the baby might just get thrown out with the bath water.

The section of the report on the impact of e-commerce is interesting. Just to quote one statistic, 90% of respondents' organizations have a Website; but 57% of them said they were not used to assist sales.

It is a valuable study that deserves to be repeated on a regular basis. *Link*: as "*Winning Business*" below.

JOURNALS

Winning Business – www.quest-media.com

This is a good magazine that ranges wide across sales and sales management issues. It is the only substantial mainstream journal published for sales managers and directors in the UK and is produced in association with The Institute of Professional Sales.

Sales Director – www.saleszone.co.uk

This is also useful and has very much the style and format of something like the journal *Management Today*.

Sales & Marketing Management – www.salesandmarketing.com

The main US magazine on the subject, broader than solely sales management and containing useful material.

Sales & Marketing Professional

This is the journal linked to the Institute of Sales & Marketing Management. Somehow this has always remained in the shadow of the main institutes. Its base is sales, but it seems to think marketing is more sexy and positions itself "higher."

All the above are specific, but it is worth bearing in mind that, as selling is an essential part of the marketing mix, marketing journals feature articles on selling and sales management from time to time. The Library at the Chartered Institute of Marketing will produce lists of recent articles on request, though there is a charge to non-members.

FILMS

Training films have traditionally been a good way to introduce or reinforce messages about sales technique, and the Video Arts Group – producing what will probably be forever known as the "John Cleese Films" – is a predominant producer. Though actor John Cleese has not been involved in any substantial way for a while, their own – almost always humorous – films are the core of their range. They also distribute various American products and have a range of e-learning products involving everything from CD-ROMs to DVDs available. Such films are worth using in a variety of settings – courses, conferences or sales meetings – and a good way to revisit and reinforce topics; often a number of films come at a subject in different ways keeping it fresh and avoiding repetition. It may be useful to request regular information from film producers to keep up to date with what is available. Most are available for purchase or rental.

www.videoarts.com

The boxed paragraph which follows (adapted from *Developing Your Staff*, Patrick Forsyth, Kogan Page) is included to provide a little advice on film use, which benefits from some care and preparation.

Using training films

First, what not to do. Films should not be regarded as an easy option: just drag people together, stick on a film and say – *look and listen*. So, how do you get the most from training films?

Selecting the right film

Let us assume that the topic is decided. You know that you want people to develop a certain skill and want to find a film on that subject. There are not so many providers and it does not take long to check catalogs and Websites or to telephone offices and check what is available. If there is a film that seems suitable, you will want to be able to assess it – is it any good? – is it suitable for *your people*? Consider:

» *the provider*: to some degree the standard (and style) of what you will get can be gauged by the company producing or distributing the film although even films from the big, well-known operators may vary a little in standard, this is a good first measure;

» *the film quality*: given the standard of what people are used to seeing in the cinema and on television, a minimum standard is probably necessary. Though this is not to say that simpler things cannot be useful; one of my own "most-used" films consists of live action, real people filmed doing real things, with no script or expensive production values – but it makes some good, clear points and is a valuable training resource (see chapter 01.10.07); and

» *the message*: how the film puts over its message is vital. If it tries to do too much in a short time for instance, it may not succeed. If it allows humor to submerge the message, this too may dilute its effectiveness. Not least does its style match your circumstances? Will your people be able to identify with characters and circumstances in the film? Does the message match the kind of way the topic needs to be dealt with in your organization?

You can get some advice from catalogs or recommendations from colleagues, but there is no substitute for seeing for yourself. Most providers have systems for previewing that work well and the time this takes, and even the small cost sometimes involved, is worthwhile. You need to plan to use not just a film, but a suitable film.

Using the film

The first thing to note is that using a training film is not an opportunity to train without effort. Most films are not designed to do a complete job unsupported. At the very least they need topping and tailing, more often they are most effective when incorporated into a session, albeit this can sometimes be a short one.

Usually a film is supplied with training notes, a booklet or guide to its use. These should always be studied. They do not need to be followed slavishly, their suggestions for sessions can be changed, lengthened, shortened or otherwise amended. But they can be useful. For example, they may help clarify exactly why a film is being used – the role it will play. This can vary. It may be to:

» introduce a topic;
» summarize key issues;
» crack through the core content, the essential principles of something;
» spark discussion; and
» link to a particular internal situation.

Whatever you do it must be clear. The film should help you meet your training objectives and it should be clear how it will do so and what role it will play (and this needs to be made clear too to the group). You can usefully plan film use specifically and systematically following something like the following sequence:

» always watch the film through yourself ahead of the session;
» read the accompanying material;
» make notes of anything you need to mention, emphasize or explain to the group;

» decide how the training points made in the film link to the totality of what you want to achieve;
» list ways in which the film can link to participation or exercises, classically noting questions that the group should address; and
» link your thinking into your overall preparation of the whole session.

It is worth thinking just a little about the physical use of a film. Set things up so that everyone can see. You may want to dim the lights, but not too much if people have to make notes. Remember that some films are designed to be seen in several parts, or have a separate summary section at the end allowing you to return to key points at the end of a session.

Note: certain films are designed in a way that links to individual study (particularly those available on CD-ROM). While introduction and briefing may still be necessary, subsequent solo study may sometimes work well from a time standpoint, for example allowing individual members of a department to see the film without the operational disruption of a group session.

The style of the film will allow different forms of training to stem from it.

» Case study based films allow one form of discussion, for example extending the scenario or varying elements of it in discussion - *what would have happened if that had not been the reaction when* . . .
» Behaviorally based films may allow more analysis of how people react, or even allow links to be made to real people in your own company.
» The classic wrong way/right way film style in which characters perform badly (exhibiting the dangers), learn lessons and then perform better (exhibiting the strengths of using correct technique), allow both aspects to be reviewed or discussed.

Stop/start use

As an example of method linked to the form of a film, consider the good way/bad way film further. By showing the film in parts it can be alternated with discussion, asking:

» what went wrong and why?
» how could matters have been handled differently?
» what are the principles involved to ensure success?

Then the "right way" part can be shown and separate discussion can follow that. Role play could be organized to extrapolate the situations portrayed in the film with members of the group extending the film characters' roles.

PROFESSIONAL BODIES

Chartered Institute of Marketing – www.cim.co.uk

This is listed first as a prime source of reference. As an overall summary they describe themselves thus:

"The Chartered Institute of Marketing (CIM) is the professional body for marketing, with over 60,000 members worldwide.

"Founded in 1911, it has been instrumental in elevating marketing to a recognised, respected and chartered profession.

"It is the only marketing body able to award Individual Chartered Marketer status to eligible members. Chartered Marketer status is a professional standard which reflects an individual's commitment to developing their professional skills in an increasingly competitive marketplace.

"As an examining body for over 60 years, the Institute's Certificates and Postgraduate Diploma (DipM) are internationally recognised qualifications, available through a worldwide network of educational institutions and distance learning providers."

In context here it is worth mentioning that CIM offer various services.

» Career development services: which include a range of information in booklet form or downloadable from their Website, a Career Advice Line (Tel: 01628 427322), a Career Counseling service (run in collaboration with Connaught Executive via a network of 25 offices around the country: tel: 01628 427322 initially) and two routes for those seeking new jobs. The first is JobFocus accessed through the

Institute's Website and is available to all, the second (for members only) is the Job Vacancy Database run with Quantum Consulting Group and accessed via: www.cim.co.uk/membership-net

» The library and information service.
» The qualifications they themselves offer.
» The network of branches: these mean no one is far from a local source of information and networking (there are a number of overseas branches also and the Institute links with the European Marketing Confederation with associate bodies in 24 countries within and outside the European Union (total membership is more than 300,000); their Website is www.emc.be
» CIM Direct: a source of business books for purchase.

In addition the Institute is the parent body for the Institute of Sales Professionals, which undertakes a parallel role to its parent, focusing solely on the sales function, and has its own Website: www.iops.co.uk

And CAM Foundation (Communication, Advertising and Marketing) which is the umbrella body for qualifications across the various marketing disciplines – www.camfoundation.com

Note: *while this is a source of value to all, you should note that some of the services listed above are available only to Members of the Institute.*

The Marketing Society – www.marketing-society.org.uk

Describes itself as, "*The premier organization in the UK for senior marketing professionals and general managers of marketing oriented companies.*" It states its purpose as: to provide access to the best network for the leading edge ideas and practice and to inspire and support Society members by encouraging debate and contact between them. It is a long established and well respected body (with something of a bias towards FMCG companies; it has a quarterly journal *Market Leader*).

Ten Steps To Making Sales Management Work

Some activities and approaches are more significant in creating results than others. Chapter 10 looks at ten key areas; all focused on creating sales management success and thus sales excellence.

- » Vision
- » Market focus
- » Setting clear guidelines
- » Assembling a top flight team
- » Spending time with the team
- » Actively motivating
- » Good communications
- » Creating sales excellence
- » Innovating
- » Active leadership

"Dealing with customers takes knowledge, time and patience – after all, if sales people don't have that, they should look for another line of work."

Lee Iacocca, former CEO of Chrysler Motors

This section is not a conventional summary. It does not simply reiterate the key tasks highlighted in the earlier section The state of the art, rather it emphasizes 10 areas all of which, albeit in different ways, are fundamental to making a success of the sales management job. They are not commented on in order of priority and, though there is some logic to the sequence, there is also some overlap.

We begin with an area that has a great deal stemming from one word.

1. THE SUCCESSFUL SALES MANAGER MUST HAVE VISION

One aspect of the sales job is also an inherent danger. There is a necessary focus on the day to day activity. Sales people make one call at a time. They must alternate between time spent with an individual customer and time spent preparing to see the next; and the preparation must lead to a precise tailoring of approach next time with every customer needing individual treatment. It can be a rather relentless process. In one direction attention is necessary on their company and their products or services, and all the attendant detail. In the other the focus is on the market, customers and competition.

It is all too easy to get locked into a rather introspective (and, worse, repetitive) mode of operation where considered approaches are replaced by an "automatic pilot" style approach. This can become pedestrian, as well as being seen by customers as standard and losing their sympathy on those grounds alone.

The wider scale of operations should influence the day to day. Seeing the full scope of what must be achieved will enliven performance and approach, keeping it fresh and ensuring it is well tailored *every* time a prospect or customer is seen.

If the sales manager does not put over a clear vision, then probably no one will do so. To enthuse the team in this way, the manager must him or her self have:

» a clear overall and *strategic* view of the business;
» real involvement with marketing and senior management;
» time to spend at this level, which should be focused on key issues;
» the ability to encapsulate the current and future view of the way forward so that communicating it makes sense; and
» An ongoing commitment to keeping this view up to date and an open mind to make it possible to do so.

Sales people will always work more effectively when they see their job in the context of a broad, worthwhile and exciting intention. Making this view possible will not distract them from the day to day, it will put them in a position to undertake their day to day tasks well.

2. THE SUCCESSFUL SALES MANAGER MUST BE MARKET FOCUSED

This may sound obvious, but it is all too easy for a sales manager to become an administrator (in the worst sense of the word), with a largely introspective view of their work. Bogged down in this way they tend to adopt an attitude that sales people should be entirely self sufficient and leave them to "get on with it."

All external contact is vital.

» *With customers*. Sales managers should not spend too much of their time selling. And further, they should not spend time selling in situations where they do so – perhaps with "difficult" or "important" customers – because "no one else on the team is up to it." What sort of team is that? But they need to keep their selling skills sharp, and they need to do enough to give sufficient first hand feedback of customers' demands, expectations and views. Only on the basis of experience and information so obtained will they be able to manage effectively, and will what they do be credible to the team?
» *With competitors*. Or indeed with any outside agency that can provide information about how selling should be conducted in future. This is a process of constant questioning – what is happening elsewhere in terms of product development, technological change or with competitive organizations themselves and the way they work?

All the methods of operation that managers must create and maintain in the sales area must be right *externally* – nothing must be done solely for internal convenience and ultimately it is the interface with the customer that is the arbiter of success; the right product, sold and supported in the right way.

3. THE SUCCESSFUL SALES MANAGER MUST SET CLEAR GUIDELINES

Sales people will never maximize their performance if they are not sure what they should be doing. Even a smidgen of doubt is too much. Everything from job descriptions to operational guidelines must be crystal clear. Nowhere is this more important than with targets, goals, standards and any mandatory operational procedures.

These must be:

» soundly and realistically based. No sales person will bust a gut trying to achieve something that is manifestly unachievable or silly;
» challenging. This is not incompatible with "sound and realistic"; it is part of what makes life at the sharp end interesting; and
» underpinned with suitable support. If orders are delivered late, quality control is poor or necessary sales aids are either not provided or inadequate, then the challenge of targets will quickly turn into resentment of them.

First, clarity in all these areas provides a sound foundation upon which a sales team can operate. Additionally, the sales manager who is *seen* to be clear and well organized about such things will always command most respect – and that in turn means more of their influence will be followed.

Moving even closer to the actual management of the team, the next area is clearly a prerequisite of success.

4. THE SUCCESSFUL SALES MANAGER HAS A TOP FLIGHT TEAM

Recruitment and selection were commented on earlier. Finding the right people is crucial and often not easy. So, the successful manager must:

» be clear about the profile of person required;
» set high standards and stick with them; a sales team has no place for passengers or "poor relations"; and
» link to, and sometimes fight for, the ability to give the right rewards. It is such a cliché but the phrase "if you pay peanuts, you get monkeys" is also a truism.

All this means a willingness to undertake any recruitment activity on a sound and thorough basis, and links back to clarity about such things as job descriptions. It takes time but attention to detail – good job advertisements, comprehensive application forms, painstaking interviewing, and a firm resolution not to resort to inappropriate, untested amateur psychology – is paramount at every stage. Then hire when you are sure and reject if you are not; people very rarely prove better than your hopes and a wrong decision in this area can be costly in many, many ways – from lost sales and muddled records to tarnished images and weakened customer relationships. It can take a long time to sort out the damage, certainly much longer than taking a little more time to make the right appointment.

5. THE SUCCESSFUL SALES MANAGER SPENDS TIME WITH THEIR TEAM

As a category, sales managers tend to have broad responsibilities. They get involved in all sorts of things from promotion to general management duties. Yet many – most – of the core sales management tasks demand that time is spent with the sales team, both individually and as a group.

Such time is crucial to the ongoing direction of sales activity. Here we divide the tasks into two broad categories.

» A key role is development. Skills must be created and maintained at a standard of excellence. Further the precise way in which skills must be deployed changes, so a constant process of amendment, and to a degree experimentation, is necessary to ensure that selling is done in a way that matches individual customers and the moment. The evaluation, counseling, mentoring and link with other development activities all take time. But it is time well spent. Ultimately sales people must be almost entirely self-sufficient. There is no way the manager can be with everybody on their every call. Time spent on joint calling is *not* to improve those few calls on which this happens, it is to enable the sales person to improve *all* those calls when they operate alone. All the various activities that contribute to this process are key. The numbers back this up. Even a small team of say 10 people may be making some 10,000 calls each year – management's job is to create excellence in them all; or, perhaps more accurately, to help the team do this.

» The second area worth highlighting is communications. Apart from the development job mentioned above, communication should take a major part of a sales manager's time. This is re-visited as point 7.

6. THE SUCCESSFUL SALES MANAGER ACTIVELY MOTIVATES

Fact: the sales force is more likely to perform well when they are well motivated. They will only be well motivated if attention is given to this on a regular basis. It is not a matter of throwing money at it, or having a complex incentive scheme and believing no more needs to be done. Saying "Well done" is as important as the many more complex things that are also needed (and, ask yourself – *have I said "Well done" often enough lately?*).

Motivation needs:

» *consideration*: unthinking or routine management will miss opportunities;
» *variety*: the changes need ringing, different things doing at different times and for different people;
» *time*: and this must not be skimped; enough said;
» *to be ongoing*: motivation is best delivered through the whole management job, not in little "motivational bursts" arranged to get it out of the way and free up time for more important things; and
» *tailoring*: just as selling must be matched to customers, so motivation must be matched to the kind of sales team involved – even to the individuals. Certainly it is important for the manager not to be censorious (i.e. remember that what is important to you may not be the same as what is important to your staff).

Motivation matters. Most of what needs doing costs little beyond some thought and some time. If people see their job as important, interesting – fun – they will work harder, and more constructively and it will show in their results.

7. THE SUCCESSFUL SALES MANAGER IS A GOOD COMMUNICATOR

Communication is ubiquitous to management. Motivation, above, consists largely of communication. Communication must be:

» *Clear*: consider just how often communications problems occur in organizations. Sometimes they cause a momentary hiccup, on other occasions breakdown is the word that describes things best and serious consequences can result. The main problem is over-confidence; everyone thinks they are a good communicator, indeed often we think that communication is easy. It is not. There are principles here worthy of study, certainly communicating well needs care, consideration and time. Errors often occur in an unthinking rush. The wrong word is chosen or the right word omitted.
» *Understandable*: this means a little more than just clear. Things must be put in the right frame of reference for people, not assuming they know more than they do, for example, or that they have experience which in fact they do not.
» *Persuasive*: often it is not just a question of telling people – we need to persuade. This is simply, or perhaps not so simply, the skills of selling applied internally. As such sales managers should be good at this; though again this will not happen automatically. The old rule of "engaging the brain before the mouth" makes sense for us all.
» *Not secretive*: this may seem either a minor point or to go without saying, but the isolation of sales people mean any apparent unnecessary secretiveness is likely to be strongly resented. Tell people what is going on and how it affects them.

Particular activities here include the following.

» *Sales meetings*: the opportunity to get the team together may be infrequent, but they are important – and often their effectiveness is low, these represent a significant opportunity to inform and encourage. They deserve time being spent in preparation to get them right.

» *Motivation*: in all its forms. The essence of this is that it is ongoing, a matter of detail, and again takes time. The right incentive scheme may be important, but so too are the small exchanges that make up the continuity of contact between the sales manager and his team. It is clearly wrong, and something I often hear on sales courses, when a sales person says: "The only time I ever see my manager is when something is wrong."

» *Appraisal*: formal appraisal is mentioned as an example of something that combines a number of elements: evaluation, motivation, planning and more. Again this seems too often to be skimped. Sales people should look forward to their appraisals, finding them constructive and this should, in turn, foster an overall constructive and productive management/sales relationship.

Communication, and you will be able to think of many other examples of how it is used and how it is important, provides the oil that lubricates the whole sales management process and with it the sales activity that it prompts.

8. THE SUCCESSFUL SALES MANAGER CREATES SALES EXCELLENCE

The question of development has already been mentioned, in Number 5 above, as a major example of where a sales manager must spend significant time. The process of defining what must be done, keeping that up to date, making sure that every member of the team can operate as required and *putting them in a position to evaluate and fine-tune their own performance* is vital. A series of activities contribute to this:

» *field training*: the whole process of working with people in the field – evaluating, counseling and generally working with people to help fine-tune performance;

» *sales meetings*: mentioned above, where a great deal of development work can be conducted quickly and easily with the whole group together;

» *formal training*: including e-learning and other alternatives to "class-room training"; and
» *appraisals*: formal appraisal systems, already mentioned, have a very direct link with development.

The above, and a whole series of other inputs, from having lunch with a sales person and talking shop to devices such as audio or video newsletters, all contribute. It is an ongoing process and the first step to making it work is clear definition of the sales job.

This needs to be entirely job and organization specific, but general overviews can be helpful here too. For instance the following comes from *McCormack on Selling*, the book written by Mark McCormack, the American sports marketing consultant and commentator:

"The qualities that I believe make a good salesman:
- believe in your product
- believe in yourself
- see a lot of people
- pay attention to timing
- listen to the customer – but realize that what the customer wants is not necessarily what he or she is telling you
- develop a sense of humor
- knock on old doors
- ask everyone to buy
- follow up after the sale with the same aggressiveness you demonstrated before the sale
- use common sense

"I have no illusions that I'm breaking new ground with this list. These are essential, self-evident, universal qualities that all sales people know in their heads – if not in their hearts."

Secondly, with the job clearly in mind, the team must be persuaded that development is natural, necessary, not an affront to their compe-tence – and thus be made acceptable, indeed desirable. A sales team that recognize they need to learn and want to move their expertise ahead is always going to have the edge on people who think they know it all and see selling as something to be applied by rote.

9. THE SUCCESSFUL SALES MANAGER INNOVATES

It cannot be said too often that sales, indeed marketing of which it is a part, is dynamic. Change is the order of the day. A quotation from management writers Robert Kriegal and David Brant puts it powerfully: "*When you're through changing, you're through. Change is a process, not a goal; a journey, not a destination.*"

This is a philosophy any sales manager (any manager?) must take on board. Essentially it necessitates:

» *recognition of change*: in all aspects of the job there is a duty to watch out for changes which impinge on you and opportunities to change for the better – better still to anticipate change. Being ahead of the trend may be a factor that helps create differentiation between you and competitors;

» *an open mind*: a willingness to review the options, to experiment (perhaps to make a few mistakes along the way) but one way or another to take if necessary radical or less obvious options if that is what will produce the desired effect; and

» *decisiveness*: decisions need to be made. Good sales managers do not spend their life sitting on the fence, and nothing demotivates sales people more than managers who acknowledge situations, promise to sort it out – and then do nothing.

This applies to every aspect of sales management. It is as important in a sense to make changes simply to update a reporting system (something that might improve productivity – less time to complete – and the precision of information gathering), as it is to make radical changes, perhaps to the way the sales activity is organized. Certainly small refinements in selling approach may be able to influence sales results significantly.

10. THE SUCCESSFUL SALES MANAGER ACTIVELY LEADS

Leadership goes beyond simple management. If management is regarded, perhaps somewhat simplistically, as organizing people and their activities, then leadership is inspiring and driving them.

As management guru Tom Peters said (in a Foreword to *The Leadership Challenge*, James M. Kouzes and Barry Z. Posner Jossey Bass Wiley)

"Leadership, many have said, is different from management. Management is mostly about 'to do' lists – can't live without them! Leadership is about tapping the wellsprings of human motivation – and about the fundamental relations with one's fellows."

Or, as Peter Drucker put it succinctly and much earlier: "*Management is doing things right; leadership is doing the right things.*"

Leadership comes, in part at least, from the sum total of the management tasks reviewed here being well executed. A good sales manager, giving time, consideration and attention to detail to the tasks they must address will find themselves leading. If there is a less definable "spark" beyond that which marks out those with leadership qualities then it is perhaps simply that they *care*: about what they do, about their organization and making it successful – and, above all, about their people.

Success here has effects inside and outside the organization. Selling is, as has been said, dynamic. Customers are demanding and fickle. The right approach – precisely the right approach – must be deployed customer by customer, meeting by meeting, day by day. Management can, and must, make a difference ensuring that sales is working effectively. When this is done it makes a difference in the marketplace; and that is the only source of all revenue and profit.

From that thought a final note on which to end is struck by quoting Mark McCormack, the American sports marketing consultant. He said in his book *McCormack on Selling*:

"I've never bought anything from sales people who didn't know their product and yet I have bought things I didn't know I needed from people who did."

Good sales people make the difference; good managers create sales excellence.

Frequently Asked Questions (FAQs)

Q1: What is the core role of sales management?

A: See Chapter 1, What is sales management?.

Q2: What are the key tasks sales management must address?

A: See Chapter 6, The state of the art.

Q3: How is modern technology affecting sales management?

A: See Chapter 4, The e-dimension.

Q4: How did sales management come to its present state?

A: See Chapter 4, The evolution of sales management.

Q5: What standards should I set?

A: See Chapter 6, The state of the art – control.

Q6: What changes should I anticipate in the role?

A: See Chapter 9, Resources – the future of selling.

Q7: How do you maximize the effectiveness of sales management?

A: See Chapter 7, In practice.

Q8: How does a sales manager need to think about their tasks and priorities to make a real difference?

A: See Chapter 7, In practice – good ideas.

Q9: How do I find out more and keep up to date?

A: See Chapter 9, Resources.

Q10: What are the priority approaches for a successful sales manager?

A: See Chapter 10, Ten steps to making sales management work.

Acknowledgments

I can claim no credit for the origination of the unique format of the series of which this work is a part. So thanks are due to those at Capstone who did so, and for the opportunity they provided for me to play a small part in so significant and novel a publishing project.

I would like also to thank Mike Wilson, founder of the consultancy and training group Marketing Improvements, of which I was a Director before setting up my own organization. He created a unique and stimulating working environment without which I would never have got involved in marketing in the way that I have done. The example of his own writing, and his personal encouragement to me, played a large part in my writing – now on a variety of marketing and management matters. Specifically, I am pleased to acknowledge his agreement to allow me to plunder the ideas and thinking in his book *Managing a Sales Force* (Gower) in working on this one.

Patrick Forsyth
Touchstone Training & Consultancy
28 Saltcote Maltings
Maldon
Essex
United Kingdom

Index